The Bible, Simplified

Learn the story. Live the story.

EIGHT SESSIONS WITH VIDEO ACCESS

Zach Windahl
with Andrea Ramsay

The Bible, Simplified Study Guide

Published in Grand Rapids, Michigan, by HarperChristian Resources. HarperChristian Resources is a registered trademark of HarperCollins Christian Publishing, Inc.

Requests for information should be sent to customercare@harpercollins.com.

ISBN 978-0-310-17409-7 (softcover)
ISBN 978-0-310-17410-3 (ebook)

HarperChristian Resources titles may be purchased in bulk for church, business, fundraising, or ministry use. For information, please e-mail ResourceSpecialist@ChurchSource.com.

First Printing May 2025 / Printed in the United States of America

Contents

A Note from Zach

Have you ever thought about what the Bible actually is? Or have you just accepted it to be the holy book of Christianity?

If I asked you to tell me the storyline of the Scriptures, could you do it? Or if I said there were sixty-six books within the Bible, would you know why? Or what they were?

The Bible is complex. It's intricate. It can be confusing if you don't understand its organization or the literary tools its authors used.

I get it. I've been there. It's far easier to just go to church on Sunday and be inspired by your pastor and everyone there than to put in the work yourself. But that leaves you missing out on so much.

You don't want to do that anymore. That's why you're doing this study. You're taking a step in the other direction and committing to learning the Bible.

God has given you the Bible as a how-to guide for making the most out of life. As A. W. Tozer once said, "The Word of God well understood and religiously obeyed is the shortest route to spiritual perfection. And we must not select a few favorite passages to the exclusion of others. Nothing less than a whole Bible can make a whole Christian."[1]

The Bible should be your lifeline. You need to study it as if you needed it to breathe.

The Bible is the most beautiful literary work the world has ever known. I call it a "literary work" because the Bible isn't just a single book. It's a collection of books that explore the interactions between God and humanity, laying the groundwork for why we exist and what we are called to be. These books tell an interwoven story of how God is using a specific group of people to bring his kingdom to the world. That's why it's so helpful to have a little historical context. The Bible isn't the type of book you can read one time and then be good for the rest of your life. No matter how many times you read it, you'll never understand it all.

And that's okay.

Studying Scripture should become a lifelong endeavor. You should read it and study it and talk about it and think about it as much as you can. The Bible is one of the most complex books in the world. You'll never learn everything about it, but you should develop a passion for it unlike anything else. As Deuteronomy 6:7 says, "Talk about [Scripture] when you sit at home and when you walk along the road, when you lie down and when you get up." God wants to be at the forefront of our minds, and he wants to speak to us through the Bible.

— **Zach Windahl**

How to Use This Guide

The Bible can be an intimidating work of literature. It's long. It's full of stories, people, places, and traditions with which you are likely unfamiliar. Maybe you've always shied away from studying it because of this. Or maybe you've tried to study the Bible in the past but lacked the context needed to fully understand it. Regardless of where you are in your relationship with Scripture, know that it is for you, and you don't need a seminary degree to study it.

God has not hidden himself from you. He reveals himself to you through nature, other people, and his Word. When you study the Bible, you are studying who God is, his plans for your life, and his plan for the world: to bring his kingdom to earth. This is the purpose of this study—to help you better understand God's Word so you can help further God's kingdom on earth.

Before you begin, know that there are a few ways you can go through this material. You can experience this study with others in a group (such as a Bible study, Sunday school class, or other gathering), or you can go through the content on your own. Either way, the videos are available to view at any time by following the instructions provided with this study guide.

Group Study

Each of the sessions in this study is divided into two parts: (1) a group study section, and (2) a personal study section. The group study section provides a basic framework for opening your time together, getting the most out of the video content, and discussing the key ideas presented in the teaching. Each session includes the following:

- **Welcome:** A short opening note about the topic of the session for you to read on your own before you meet as a group.
- **Connect:** A few icebreaker questions to get you and your group members thinking about the topic and interacting with each other.

- **Watch:** An outline of the key points covered in each video teaching along with space for you to take notes as you watch each session.

- **Discuss:** Questions to help you and your group reflect on the teaching material presented and apply it to your lives.

- **Respond:** A short personal exercise to help reinforce the key ideas.

- **Pray:** A closing prayer for the group as you conclude the session.

If you are doing this study in a group, make sure you have your own copy of the study guide so you can write down your thoughts, responses, and reflections in the space provided—and so you can have access to the videos via streaming. You will also want to have a copy of *The Bible, Simplified* book, as reading it alongside this guide will provide you with deeper insights. (See the notes at the beginning of each group session and personal study section on which chapters of the book you should read before the next group session.)

Finally, keep these points in mind:

- **Facilitation:** If you are doing this study in a group, appoint someone to serve as a facilitator. This person will be responsible for starting the video and keeping track of time during discussions and activities. If *you* have been chosen for this role, there are some resources in the back of this guide that can help you lead your group through the study.

- **Faithfulness:** Your group is a place where growth can happen as you reflect on the Bible, ask questions, and learn what God is doing in other people's lives. For this reason, be fully committed and attend each session so you can build trust and rapport with the other members.

- **Friendship:** The goal of any small group is to serve as a place where people can share, learn about God, and build friendships. So seek to make your group a welcoming place. Be honest about your thoughts and feelings, but also listen carefully to everyone else's thoughts, feelings, and opinions. Keep anything personal that your group members share in confidence so that you can create a community where people can be challenged and grow spiritually.

If you are going through this study on your own, read the opening Welcome section and reflect on the questions in the Connect section. Watch the video and use the outline provided to help you take notes. Finally, personalize the questions and exercises in the Discuss and Respond sections. Close by recording any requests you want to pray about during the week.

Personal Study

The personal study is for you to work through on your own during the week. Each exercise is designed to help you explore the key ideas you uncovered during your group time and delve into passages of Scripture that will help you apply those principles to your life. Go at your own pace, doing a little each day—or tackle the material all at once. Remember to spend a few moments in silence to listen to whatever God might be saying to you.

Note that if you are doing this study as part of a group, and you are unable to finish (or even start) these personal studies for the week, you should still attend the group time. Be assured that you are still wanted and welcome even if you don't have your "homework" done. The group studies and personal studies are intended to help you hear what God wants you to hear and learn how to apply what he is saying to your life. So . . . as you go through this study, be listening for him to speak to you through his Word and reveal how you can start bringing his kingdom to earth today.

Schedule | Week 1

BEFORE GROUP MEETING	Read the introduction and chapters 1-3 in *The Bible, Simplified* Read the Welcome section (page 2)
GROUP MEETING	Discuss the Connect questions Watch the video teaching for session 1 Discuss the questions that follow as a group Do the closing exercise and pray (pages 2-6)
STUDY 1	Complete the personal study (pages 9-11)
STUDY 2	Complete the personal study (pages 13-15)
STUDY 3	Complete the personal study (pages 17-19)
CONNECT AND DISCUSS	Connect with one or two group members Discuss the follow-up questions (page 20)
CATCH UP AND READ AHEAD (before week 2 group meeting)	Read chapters 4-10 in *The Bible, Simplified* Complete any unfinished studies (page 21)

SESSION ONE

What Is the Bible?

We have the Bible available to us at all times to learn about God, connect with him, and understand what it means to live under his rule and reign, in his kingdom, here and now.

Welcome [READ ON YOUR OWN]

What is the Bible? That's a loaded question. Your answer depends on your relationship with it, how you were introduced to it, how much time you spend with it, what Christian tradition you come from, and what you've been taught about it.

There are a lot of misconceptions about the Bible. Some think it's just a long list of rules. Others think it's a bunch of old stories that have nothing to do with today. And others see it as simply another way to explain humanity and our history, like any other religious text. But the Bible is so much more.

The Bible, when you take a forty-thousand-foot view of it, is actually one beautiful, connected story about God, his kingdom, and his relationship with his people. It's a story of heartache and redemption, loss and gain, humility and strength. Within its pages are characters who reflect who we are today: people trying to do the right thing and follow God while falling short over and over again.

So, no matter what your relationship is with the Bible, know this study is for you. The *Bible* is for you. The better you understand Scripture as a whole, the better you will understand its individual passages, helping you grasp God's great love for you.

In this session, you will learn about the structure of the Bible, its authors, and its primary narrative. Having this framework in place is essential for understanding what the stories in the Bible have to do with your life, culture, and context. The more you learn about this intriguing literary work, the more you will want to return to its pages.

Connect [10 MINUTES]

If you or any of your group members don't know each other, take a few minutes to introduce yourselves. Then discuss one or both of the following questions:

- Why did you decide to join this study? What do you hope to learn?

— *or* —

- When is the first time you opened a Bible? What were your impressions of it?

Watch [25 MINUTES]

Watch the video for this session, which you can access by playing the DVD or through streaming (see the instructions provided with this guide). Below is an outline of the key points covered during the teaching. Record any key concepts that stand out to you.

OUTLINE

I. **What is in the Bible?**
   A. The Bible is more than just rules and wisdom. It's a work of literary genius.
   B. The Bible is a collection of sixty-six books divided into two sections: an Old Testament and a New Testament.
   C. The Bible is written in three different literary styles: narrative, poetry, and prose discourse.
   D. The Bible has forty different authors and was written over 1,500 years.

II. **How should you read the Bible?**
   A. "Pray before opening." Trust the Holy Spirit will guide you as you read.
   B. Historical and cultural context is key when reading and understanding stories in the Bible.
   C. Ask: *Who wrote this book? Who was it written to? When was it written and why?*
   D. A Western mindset likes data and facts. An Eastern mindset likes stories and symbolism.

III. **What is the story of the Old Testament?**
   A. Adam and Eve lived in perfect union with God until they chose sin over him.
   B. God works to restore his relationship with us through people like Noah, Abraham, and Jacob.
   C. God frees his people through his servant Moses—and the promised land is established.
   D. The Israelites cycle through leaders and kings, obeying and disobeying the Lord.

IV. **What is the story of the New Testament?**
   A. Jesus showed up preaching a new way of life—a kingdom lifestyle.
   B. Jesus was executed on a Roman cross and then rose from the dead, restoring our relationship to God.
   C. Now we are called to spread this good news to the world and live under the new covenant.

NOTES

"The Bible tells the story of God's relationship with humanity and what our role on earth is."

Discuss [35 MINUTES]

Discuss what you just watched by answering the following questions.

1. The Bible is much more than a list of rules. What did you learn in this session about the Bible's structure? How does this change the way you view the Bible?

2. In the teaching segment you learned about the importance of context in the Bible. Why is context so important? What is an example of a time that you (or someone you know) read something from the Bible without context and misinterpreted it?

3. What are some of the differences between a Western mindset and an Eastern mindset? How have you experienced these differences either when reading the Bible or interacting with people from different cultures?

4. Ask someone to read Romans 5:12–14. What story is Paul referring to here? Why is it important to know about Adam and Eve and how sin entered into the world in the Old Testament in order to fully understand Jesus' story in the New Testament?

5. Ask someone to read aloud John 1:1–14. How does this story fit into the rest of Scripture? How is Jesus present in both the Old and New Testaments?

Respond [10 MINUTES]

Remember: The Bible is not a long list of rules, nor is it a collection of separate books that have nothing to do with each other. Rather, the Bible is an incredible literary feat, written over a record amount of time, with all books working together under the arch of one big story: God establishing his kingdom on earth. And the Bible is applicable to your life today. Read the following passage that reflects on this truth and answer the questions below.

> 14 But as for you, continue in what you have learned and have become
> convinced of, because you know those from whom you learned it,
> 15 and how from infancy you have known the Holy Scriptures, which
> are able to make you wise for salvation through faith in Christ Jesus.
> 16 All Scripture is God-breathed and is useful for teaching, rebuking,
> correcting and training in righteousness, 17 so that the servant of God
> may be thoroughly equipped for every good work.
>
> **2 TIMOTHY 3:14–17**

This is part of a letter that Paul wrote to a younger Jesus-follower named Timothy. Timothy's mother, Eunice, and grandmother, Lois, had raised him to know the Old Testament (see 2 Timothy 1:5). How does this context help you understand the passage?

According to Paul, what is Scripture? What can it do in you? How have you experienced this in your life?

Pray [10 MINUTES]

When it is time to close this session, take a moment to pray with your group. Pray for your time together and individually in God's Word. Pray that the Holy Spirit would reveal new and deeper truths. Finally, pray that God would give you and your group a renewed passion for the Bible.

SESSION ONE

PERSONAL STUDY

The evangelist Billy Graham said, "The Bible is not an option; it is a necessity. You cannot grow spiritually strong without it."[2] The goal of this personal study section is to help you learn more about what the Bible is and how to study it so you can grow spiritually. *How* you study matters just as much as *what* you study. These personal studies will help you explore the story of the Bible, how to understand its historical context, and why the literary styles in the Bible matter (and how to decipher them). As you work through these exercises, be sure to write down your responses to the questions, as you will be given a few minutes to share your insights at the start of the next session. If you are reading *The Bible, Simplified* alongside this study, first review the introduction and chapters 1–3 of the book.

The Bible is a collection of

66 BOOKS

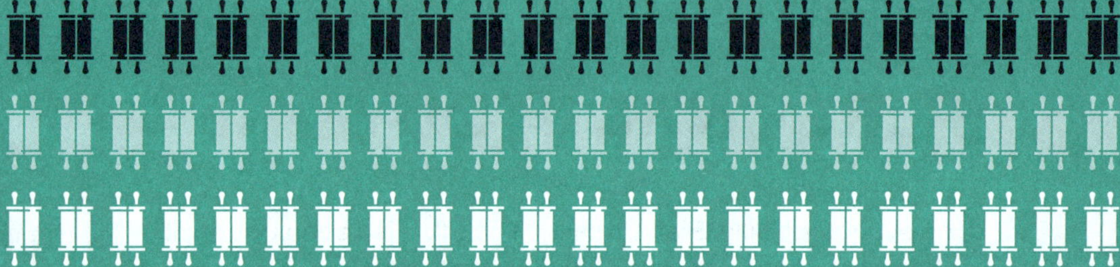

written by

40 *(or more)* **AUTHORS**

over a span of

1,500 YEARS

from

3 CONTINENTS

in

3 LANGUAGES

and all make sense in the storyline of Scripture

STUDY 1 | God and His People

Opening the Bible can feel overwhelming. Look at how small that text is! How thin the pages are. How much farther you have to go. However, if you open your Bible with a little knowledge about what it is and how it works, it will feel less daunting.

Our word *Bible* comes from the Greek word *biblia*, which means "the books."[3] This is what the Bible is—a collection of sixty-six books written in narrative, poetry, and prose. The Christian Bible is split into the Old Testament and the New Testament. The Old Testament is the original Hebrew Bible used by the Jewish people. It is comprised of thirty-nine books that were written by twenty-five (or more) authors and spans the time of Creation to around 400 BC. The New Testament is comprised of twenty-seven books penned by nine (or more) authors and primarily spans the first century AD.

The books in the Old and New Testaments *inform* one another. Understanding the Fall in Genesis, when sin entered the world, is crucial for understanding the mission of Jesus in the Gospels, when he came to redeem humanity from sin. Knowing about the enslavement of the Hebrew people in Egypt, as told in the book of Exodus, helps in understanding the freedom Christ brought to all who are enslaved in sin.

One of the major themes in the Bible is God's desire to have a relationship with us. Scripture is clear about how God feels about his people. For instance, Deuteronomy 7:9 says, "The Lord your God . . . is the faithful God, keeping his covenant of love to a thousand generations." Psalm 86:15 says, "But you, Lord, are a compassionate and gracious God, slow to anger, abounding in love and faithfulness." John 3:16 says, "For God so loved the world that he gave his one and only Son, that whoever believes in him should not perish but have eternal life."

God's love for us is a common thread in Scripture. We fall short of that love. We don't deserve it. Abraham, Moses, and Jacob were all the forefathers of the faith, but they weren't perfect. The Israelites often strayed. They broke their covenant with God again and again. So God, in his steadfast love, formed a new covenant with us through Jesus.

When you're reading this big story, Jesus' death is the climax. His resurrection is the resolution. And this part of the story doesn't just happen in the Gospels. It started at the very beginning, on page one of Genesis. Jesus is on every page. When we understand this, the Bible is more hopeful, more exciting, and much easier to understand.

SCRIPTURE: Deuteronomy 7:7–9; Psalm 86:15–17; John 3:16–17; Luke 15:11–32

OBSERVATION

1 Based on Deuteronomy 7:7–9, Psalm 86:15–17, and John 3:16–17, what is God's love like? How does this make you feel about your relationship with God?

2 How does the story in Luke 15:11–32 symbolize the kind of love that God has for all people? How does it capture the overarching theme of God's love in the Bible?

3 In this story, the father represents God, while the two sons represent different kinds of people who sin against the Lord (the rebellious and the self-righteous). How would you describe what motivates each of these characters in the story?

CHARACTER	What motivates this character?
THE FATHER	
THE YOUNGER SON	
THE OLDER SON	

How do you see parts of your own nature reflected in the story of the two sons?

APPLICATION

4 Using the following scale, how would you rate your knowledge of the Bible?

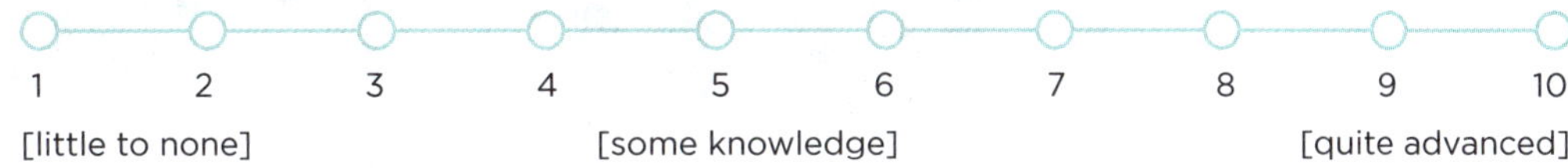

Why did you give yourself this particular rating?

5 Before this week's session, how would you have described the Bible to someone who had never heard of it? Why would you have described it that way?

PRAYER

Dear God, thank you for the Bible. Thank you for the parables, psalms, and stories inside of it. Help me understand you better as I study your Word. Reveal yourself to me so that I may accept your love and deepen my relationship with you. In Jesus' name, I pray. Amen.

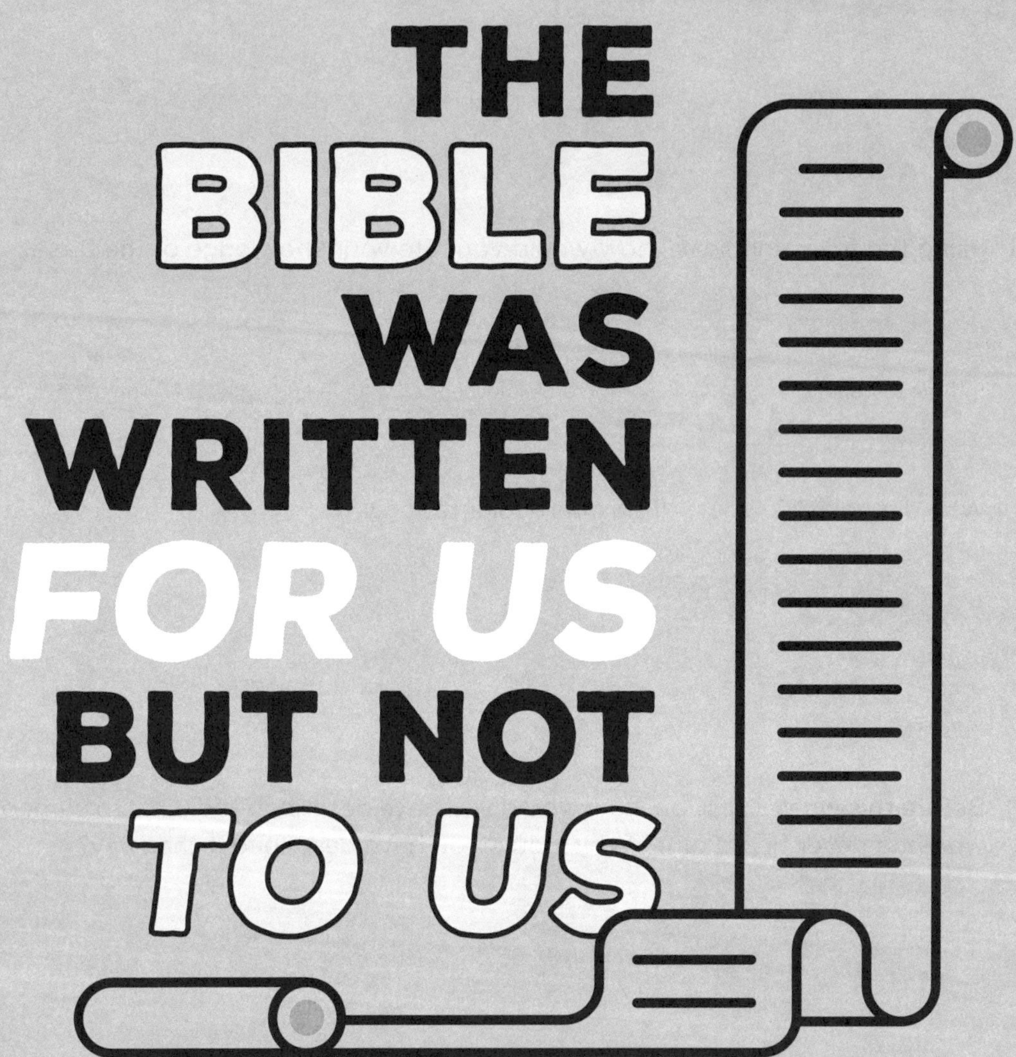
THE
BIBLE
WAS
WRITTEN
FOR US
BUT NOT
TO US

STUDY 2 | Context Is Key

Imagine starting a new TV series on episode four rather than episode one. The main characters are in conflict, but you don't know why. An undercover agent is getting closer to solving the case, but you don't know what the case is. This would be confusing, right? You would wonder what was going on, who the characters were, where they were from, and why they were motivated to do what they were doing. However, if you had started the series by watching episode one, you would know the answers to these questions.

When it comes to the Bible, overlooking historical and cultural context is kind of like starting a TV series halfway through. You miss out on a lot of crucial information that informs the story and helps it make sense. In addition, you might draw incorrect conclusions about what is happening and why. This is inconvenient with a TV show. With the Bible, it's dangerous. Misinterpreting God's Word can have serious consequences. This is why context is key.

The Bible was written *for* us, but not *to* us. This means that the authors of the Bible had a specific audience in mind when they wrote their books. Moses, who is traditionally held to be the author of Genesis, was writing to the Hebrews, who were trying to understand their history as a people group.[4] David, the author of many of the psalms, was writing personal poetry about his love for God, trust in God, and respect toward God. Paul, in his works, was generally writing to churches in places like Rome, Corinth, and Philippi.

Understanding this context will enrich your experience of the Bible. As you discover *who* wrote *what* to *whom*, and *when* and *why* it was written, you will better understand what God is trying to convey through that particular passage. For example, Jesus often compares himself to a shepherd (see John 10:11). You likely don't have much experience with shepherds and sheep, but Jesus' audience was largely agricultural. He was speaking about their day jobs. They knew what the shepherd did, and they knew the religious elite of the day considered shepherds to be members of an unclean profession.[5] Jesus was associating himself with this group! It was a snub to the religious elite—something you can only understand if you know the context.

Explore today's readings by practicing a little context work. See how this type of study can reveal even more about God's Word.

SCRIPTURE: Matthew 26:17–30; Exodus 12:1–17; John 1:29

OBSERVATION

1. The story in Matthew 26:17–30 takes place on the first day of the Festival of Unleavened Bread. Consider this as you answer the following questions.

   What took place on the first day of this festival (see verses 17–19)?

   What did the participants eat and drink at this event (see verses 26–29)?

2. The story in Matthew reveals *what* Jesus and his disciples did but not *why* they did it. For this, you need some context. So now read Exodus 12:1–17.

   What does this passage reveal about the Passover, which was the meal Jesus celebrated with his disciples (see verses 1–11)?

   What is the significance of the unleavened bread used in this meal (see verse 15)?

   Jesus said the wine used at the Passover represented his blood. What significance did blood play in the first Passover for the Israelites (see verses 12–13)?

3. The Passover can also help you understand the words of John the Baptist that you read in John 1:29. What is the significance of Jesus being "the Lamb of God"?

APPLICATION

4. When has a lack of context caused you to misinterpret something that you read in the Bible? When has context helped you understand Scripture better?

5 Below are some resources you can use to explore historical and cultural context. You have thousands of options to choose from at all sorts of price points, so it's up to you which direction to go, but this will give you a basic starter list.[6]

Historical context:
The IVP Bible Background Commentary: New Testament, edited by Craig S. Keener (Lisle, IL: InterVarsity Press, 1993).

The IVP Bible Background Commentary: Old Testament, edited by John H. Walton, et al (Lisle, IL: InterVarsity Press, 2000).

HarperCollins Bible Commentary, edited by James L. Mays (New York: HarperCollins, 2000).

New Bible Commentary, edited by Gordon J. Wenham, et al (Lisle, IL: Intervarsity Press, 1994).

Cultural context:
The New Testament in Its World: An Introduction to the History, Literature, and Theology of the First Christians, by N. T. Wright and Michael F. Bird (Grand Rapids, MI: Zondervan, 2019).

A Survey of the Old Testament, by Andrew E. Hill and John H. Walton (Grand Rapids, MI: Zondervan, 2023).

Reading the Bible with Rabbi Jesus: How a Jewish Perspective Can Transform Your Understanding, by Lois Tverberg (Grand Rapids, MI: Baker Publishing Group, 2018).

Simply Jesus, by N. T. Wright (New York: HarperCollins, 2012).

Simply Christian, by N. T. Wright (San Francisco: HarperOne, 2021).

Video series and podcasts:
That the World May Know, by Ray Vander Laan, sixteen volumes (Colorado Springs, CO: Focus on the Family; Grand Rapids, MI: HarperChristian Resources, 2006–2018).

The Bible Project (bibleproject.com), offers videos, podcasts, articles, and classes to help people experience the Bible in a way that is approachable and transformative.

PRAYER

Heavenly Father, help me understand what you're communicating in the Bible. Help me to learn how to hear your voice. Give me time and energy to dig into your Word so I can apply it to my life. I know with Scripture there is always more to learn. Amen.

Poetry
Prose

Narrative

STUDY 3 | Narrative, Poetry, and Prose

Unless you were an English nerd in school, the phrase "literary style" probably doesn't excite you. In fact, it may send you right back to your high school English class—a place you would rather *not* return to. But understanding the different literary styles in the Bible isn't simply another lecture from boring English class. It's a way to better engage with the Bible, understand it, and relate to the God who inspired it.

As you learned this week, the Bible is written in three literary styles: narrative (or story), poetry, and prose discourse. *Narrative* makes up the majority of the Bible (about 43 percent). Stories are how we best make sense of the world around us. In fact, according to neuroscience, our brains are hardwired to understand our lives and our context through story.[7] So it just makes sense that so many authors of the Bible used this literary style when writing their books.

Poetry makes up about 33 percent of the Bible. The five books of poetry in the Bible are Job, Psalms, Proverbs, Ecclesiastes, and Song of Songs. *Prose discourse* makes up about 24 percent. It includes letters (think of the books written by Paul and others in the New Testament) and speeches (like the ones by Moses featured in Deuteronomy).

You are probably drawn to one style over another. Some of us love a good story. Others are suckers for the emotional stuff—poetry that speaks to the deepest parts of us. Some enjoy the debate, discourse, and organization of a logical argument. Yet while you may *prefer* one style, *all* are needed. If the Bible were just one long argument written by Paul, you would probably get bored. If it were just one story after another, you would be missing context and application. And if it were just one epic poem written by David, you would miss the ebb and flow of characters, narrative, and plot.

Some of these styles reflect the audience of the time and what they would understand. While you may feel comfortable with the logic, data, and facts of discourse (something Paul often used for his audience), Jesus' audience would better comprehend through story, which is why he told so many parables.

Understanding the literary style of the Bible helps us understand the context in which it was written and the purpose it served. Put together, this mix of styles results in a beautiful and complex piece of literature—the depths of which we will never fully be able to explore.

SCRIPTURE: Exodus 2:23–3:12; Judges 6:1–16; Psalm 106:7–12; Hebrews 11:24–29

OBSERVATION

1. Sometimes you will find narratives in the Bible that are similar in nature. Read the stories of Moses' calling in Exodus 2:23–3:12 and Gideon's calling in Judges 6:1–16.

   What was the situation in Israel in each story (compare Exodus 2:23–25 to Judges 6:1–6)?

   What did God say to each man (compare Exodus 3:9–10 to Judges 6:15)?

   How did each man react to God's calling (compare Exodus 3:11 to Judges 6:15)?

   How did God reply to each man's objection (compare Exodus 3:12 to Judges 6:16)?

2. Sometimes you will find poetry in the Bible that recounts a story previously told. Consider Psalm 106:7–12, which refers back to a story told in Exodus 14:1–31. What is the story being retold in this psalm? Why do you think it benefited the

Israelites to have a psalm like this that reminded them of what had happened to their ancestors generations before?

3 Now consider Hebrews 11:24–29. What literary style does the author use in this passage? What is his purpose here in referring back to the story of the exodus?

APPLICATION

4 Which of the three styles used in the Bible—narrative, poetry, or prose—appeals to you the most? Why does that style especially resonate with you?

5 After studying each of these different styles, why do you think all three are essential to the Bible?

PRAYER

Lord, your Word is vast, complex, and beautiful. Thank you for inspiring the authors who wrote it to create their texts in so many unique and different ways. Give me a heart for your entire Word—even those parts that seem too difficult and complex at the moment for me to understand. Renew my passion for it daily so I never tire of opening my Bible. Amen.

CONNECT AND DISCUSS

Connect with a fellow group member and discuss some of the key insights from this session. Use any of the following prompts to help guide your discussion.

1. What did you like best from the content in this session, including both the group study and personal study? Why?

2. How has this study encouraged or inspired your exploration of the Bible?

3. How has this study challenged you and your relationship with the Bible?

4. What do you feel most excited to explore in the sessions ahead? Why?

CATCH UP AND READ AHEAD

Use this time to go back and complete any of the study and reflection questions from previous days that you weren't able to finish. Make a note below of any revelations you've had and reflect on any growth or personal insights you've gained.

Read chapters 4–10 in *The Bible, Simplified* before the next group gathering. Use the space below to make note of anything in those chapters that stands out to you, inspires you, or encourages you.

Schedule | Week 2

BEFORE GROUP MEETING	Read chapters 4–10 in *The Bible, Simplified* Read the Welcome section (page 24)
GROUP MEETING	Discuss the Connect questions Watch the video teaching for session 2 Discuss the questions that follow as a group Do the closing exercise and pray (pages 24–28)
STUDY 1	Complete the personal study (pages 31–33)
STUDY 2	Complete the personal study (pages 35–37)
STUDY 3	Complete the personal study (pages 39–41)
CONNECT AND DISCUSS	Connect with one or two group members Discuss the follow-up questions (page 42)
CATCH UP AND READ AHEAD (before week 3 group meeting)	Read chapters 11–16 in *The Bible, Simplified* Complete any unfinished studies (page 43)

SESSION TWO

Creation and Covenants

God chose to partner with individuals like Abraham who would, in return, positively influence the rest of humanity. He would make a covenant with them and hold up his end of the bargain—even if they failed on their end.

Welcome [READ ON YOUR OWN]

You are probably familiar with the Bible's opening phrase: "In the beginning . . . " (Genesis 1:1). Beginnings are hopeful. They represent opportunity. Think about a beginning you've experienced: the beginning of a job, the beginning of a marriage, the beginning of being a parent, the beginning of life in a new city. Beginnings are exciting.

Yet, more often than not, the *middle* and *end* you envisioned at the beginning won't pan out as you planned. You will encounter hardships, obstacles, and unforeseen events. It can cause you to feel nostalgic for those beginnings you had.

Genesis can feel a bit like this. The Creation story, found in the first two chapters, is a poetic tale of how God brought order to chaos, separating sky and sea and land, bringing forth fruit from the earth, and creating humans from the dust. Adam and Eve, the first man and woman, thrived in the garden of Eden, and God walked in their midst. But then a serpent, a deceitful promise, and a sinful choice led to the Fall.

Just a few verses into Genesis, everything has gone awry. The hopeful beginning has taken a terrible turn. Adam and Eve have made a choice to pursue their own way over God's, which has led to separation from him. As a result, the Lord determines to restore his relationship with his people. He makes covenants with them. But each time, his people break the covenants. So God makes a new one, and then another one.

God remains faithful, even as we do not. This is what you will explore in this session. Through Creation and covenants, God showed Adam and Eve and their descendants that he was their God and they were his people . . . no matter how far they strayed.

Connect [10 MINUTES]

If you or any of your group members don't know each other, take a few minutes to introduce yourselves. Then discuss one or both of the following questions:

- What is something that spoke to you in last week's personal study that you would like to share with the group?

— *or* —

- What covenants have you made in your life—an agreement with someone else that required you to uphold your end of the bargain?

Watch [25 MINUTES]

Now watch the video for this session. Below is an outline of the key points covered during the teaching. Record any key concepts that stand out to you.

OUTLINE

I. **What happened on each day of Creation?**
   A. Day 1: God created the heavens and earth. He separated light from darkness.
   B. Day 2: God separated the water on the earth from the water in the sky.
   C. Day 3: God created land. He created plants and fruit trees at this time.
   D. Day 4: God created the sun, moon, and stars.
   E. Day 5: God created the animals in the sea and the birds in the air.
   F. Day 6: God created all the animals that live on land. He also created humans.
   G. Day 7: God rested, not because he was tired, but because all was complete.

II. **How did sin enter into the world?**
   A. Adam and Eve lived in harmony with God and his creation in Eden.
   B. God gave them a choice—to trust in his plan or to make their own choice.
   C. Adam and Eve chose to take things into their own hands (the Fall of man).

III. **What was the Great Flood in the Bible?**
   A. The world became so evil that God determined to wipe out humanity.
   B. God commanded Noah to build a massive boat for his family and the bloodline of each animal.
   C. It rained for forty days and forty nights, destroying everything on the earth. Yet God spared Noah, his family, and the rest of the inhabitants of the ark.

IV. **What are the covenants in Scripture?**
   A. Noahic Covenant: God promised to never destroy humanity again.
   B. Abrahamic Covenant: God promised to give Abraham more descendants than he could count along with a land in which they could live.
   C. Mosaic Covenant: A two-sided covenant in which God promised to bless his people if they remained faithful to his law.
   D. Davidic Covenant: God promised he would send a new King from David's descendants to benefit humankind whose kingdom would last forever.
   E. New Covenant: God promised that whoever believes in Jesus and accepts his sacrifice will become a part of his new covenantal family.

V. **Who were the patriarchs?**
   A. Abraham and Sarah traveled to a special land God had prepared for them.
   B. Isaac was the son of God's promise.
   C. Jacob was a son of Isaac. From his lineage came the twelve tribes of Israel.

NOTES

CREATION
PATRIARCHS
Creation (Eden)
The Fall
The Flood
Abrahamic Covenant

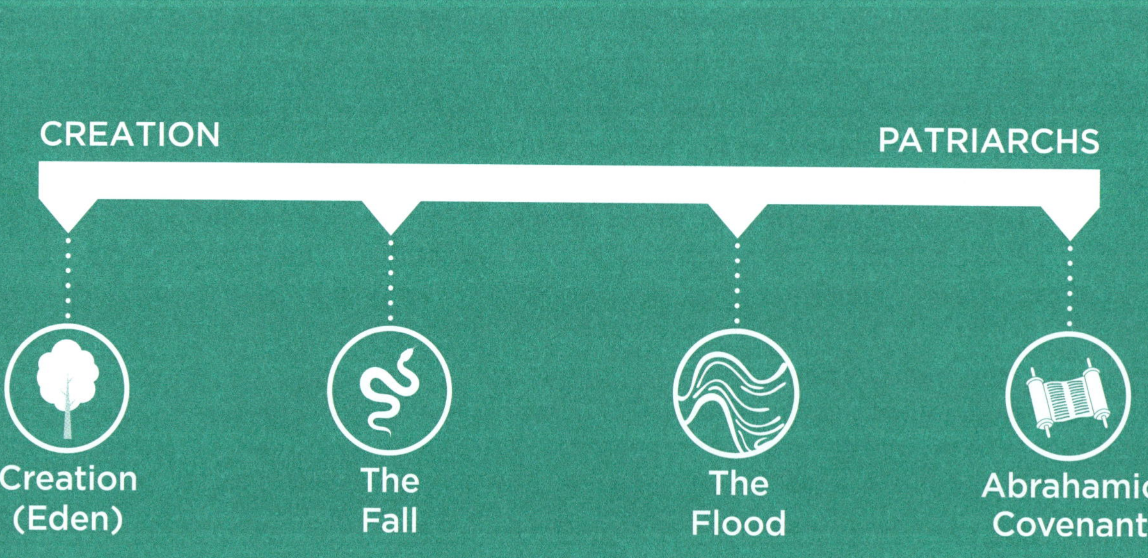

Discuss [35 MINUTES]

Discuss what you just watched by answering the following questions.

1. The Creation account is more than just God creating animals, plants, and people. What is the significance of God creating *order* out of *chaos*? What does this say about his nature?

2. Ask someone to read Genesis 3:1–7. How was the serpent able to convince Adam and Eve to disobey God? What were they actually choosing when they did this?

3. Ask someone to read aloud Genesis 8:20–22. What kind of covenant does this represent? How would you describe what God was promising to do (or not do) in this covenant?

4. Now ask someone to read Genesis 12:1–8. What kind of covenant does this represent? What similarities do you see between this covenant and the Noahic covenant?

5. How does learning about Creation and covenants help you understand the rest of the Bible? How does it help you understand your relationship with God?

Respond [10 MINUTES]

Knowing how the biblical story begins is important for understanding the rest of the Bible and God's covenant relationship with us—one that resulted in the New Covenant of Jesus Christ. Jesus was the ultimate covenant . . . the ultimate tie that connects us with the Father forever. Read the following passage that reflects this truth and answer the questions below.

> 13 The blood of goats and bulls and the ashes of a heifer sprinkled on
> those who are ceremonially unclean sanctify them so that they are
> outwardly clean. 14 How much more, then, will the blood of Christ,
> who through the eternal Spirit offered himself unblemished to God,
> cleanse our consciences from acts that lead to death, so that we may
> serve the living God! 15 For this reason Christ is the mediator of a new
> covenant, that those who are called may receive the promised eternal
> inheritance—now that he has died as a ransom to set them free from
> the sins committed under the first covenant.
>
> **HEBREWS 9:13-15**

What is the "New Covenant" the author of Hebrews describes in this passage?

What does God promise under the New Covenant? How is it different from any of the other covenants found in the Old Testament?

Pray [10 MINUTES]

Close your session in prayer. Thank God for his covenants and his consistent desire to restore the relationship with his people. Ask him for guidance as you live out the New Covenant—one covered in grace. And ask for wisdom to show grace to others as it has been shown to you.

SESSION TWO

PERSONAL STUDY

The Old Testament is so much more than just a bunch of strange stories, obscure genealogies, and confusing rules. This ancient text is full of relevant wisdom! During this week's group time, you learned about the Creation story, the Fall (original sin), and the covenants that God made with his people. These personal studies will help you dig deeper into these topics and stories. Each one provides insight into your own relationship with God and points to the future climax of our biblical story: Jesus' life, death, and resurrection. As you work through the exercises, write down your responses to the questions, as you will be given a few minutes to share your insights at the start of the next session if you are doing this study with others. If you are reading *The Bible, Simplified* alongside this study, first review chapters 4–10 in the book.

THE WORLD OF THE PATRIARCHS

STUDY 1 | The Seed of Eve

The first poem in the Bible occurs in the first chapter in Genesis—it's a poem about how God created the world by bringing order to chaos. This is what God does. He restores order and makes things right. When things are going God's way, we feel peaceful and calm, and everything is in its right place. But when things are going humanity's way, chaos often ensues.

This is what sin did in the garden of Eden. It brought chaos to an otherwise orderly way of being—and it brought chaos to the souls of Adam and Eve. One rabbinic tradition suggests that *sin* is "losing our way or forgetting who we are for a second."[8] It is a moment in which we stray from the ordered way of things and how God intended them. When Adam and Eve sinned, they forgot who they were—image bearers of God sharing in his abundant blessings.

When have you forgotten who you are? How many times after sinning have you thought, *I just wasn't being myself in that moment*? When you sin, you *aren't* being yourself. You aren't being who God intended you to be. You've stepped out of order and into chaos. Fortunately, God has provided a way to escape the chaos. It's as easy as remembering who we are and who God is. The Bible often instructs us to do this:

> Be careful that you do not forget the Lord, who brought you out of Egypt, out of the land of slavery (Deuteronomy 6:12).
>
> Remember this, keep it in mind, take it to heart, you rebels. Remember the former things, those of long ago; I am God, and there is no other (Isaiah 46:8–9).
>
> I will remember the deeds of the Lord; yes, I will remember your miracles of long ago (Psalm 77:11).

We often think of Adam and Eve as the "original" sinners and just view that as the end of their story. However, the Bible reveals that God didn't abandon them or their descendants after they were banished from the garden of Eden. The Fall—that moment when they made a conscious choice to sin by disobeying God—was *not* the end of their story. And it's not where our story ends either. The seed of Eve is in each of us—the seed of *restoration* and *redemption*.

SCRIPTURE: Genesis 4:1–26

OBSERVATION

1. God's conversations with Cain in verses 6–16 reveal that the Lord had not abandoned the human race. Explain God's words to Cain and his response or reactions.

GOD'S WORDS TO CAIN	CAIN'S RESPONSE OR REACTION
verses 6–7:	verse 8:
verse 9:	verse 9:
verses 10–12:	verses 13–14:
verse 15:	verse 16:

2. Review verses 25–26. The Hebrew root of the name *Seth* is "foundation." The name *Enosh* means "human."[9] How do these descendants represent redemption for Adam and Eve? What glimmer of hope for humanity do we see at the end of this chapter in Genesis?

APPLICATION

3. Paul wrote, "I do not understand what I do. For what I want to do I do not do, but what I hate I do. . . . As it is, it is no longer I myself who do it, but it is sin living in me" (Romans 7:15, 17). How does this describe your situation when you fall into sin? How is sin acting like someone you are not?

4. How does the story you read in Genesis 4:1–26 make you think differently about Eve and her legacy? How does it make you think differently about yourself and your sin?

5. Take a few moments to *remember* who God is today. Write down a few characteristics that you know are true of him and the attributes he has given to you.

PRAY

Lord, may I remember who you are. May I remember who I am in you. When I fall into sin, help me to understand that isn't the nature or character that you desire for me to have. I am who you made me to be. Help me live out that truth today. In Jesus' name, amen.

Noahic

Abrahamic

Mosaic

Davidic

New

STUDY 2 | A Visual Reassurance

When a couple gets married, it is traditional for both parties to vow to remain faithful to each "for better, for worse, for richer, for poorer, in sickness and in health, until death do us part." In a business partnership, it is typical for both parties to agree to certain terms that are likely written down in a legally binding contract that prevents one from taking advantage of the other. Even in less formal agreements—like the one between a student and a teacher—one party agrees to listen to lectures and do the homework in exchange for a passing grade.

These are examples of *covenants* that we engage in every day. We are accustomed to their terms and the written and unwritten rules that uphold them. People in Old Testament times were also accustomed to covenants. However, while we mark covenants with wedding bands and signed contracts, they marked them in ways that might seem unusual to us.

For example, some covenants were made by cutting an animal (or animals) in half. Both parties would then walk through the middle of the cut animals as a symbol of the binding nature of the agreement. In Genesis 15, God used this method as visual representation of the covenant that he had made with Abraham several years before:

> [2] I will make you into a great nation,
> and I will bless you;
> I will make your name great,
> and you will be a blessing.
> [3] I will bless those who bless you,
> and whoever curses you I will curse;
> and all peoples on earth
> will be blessed through you (Genesis 12:2–3).

Abraham had begun to doubt God's promise, which prompted the Lord to instruct him to bring several animals to cut in half. However, as you will see in this study, there was something unusual in the ceremony that followed—a significant detail that represents the difference between covenants made between humans and a covenant made between a human and God. This is a detail we see again and again in the Old Testament until we reach the New Covenant through Jesus—the final covenant between humans and God.

SCRIPTURE: Genesis 15:1–21

OBSERVATION

1 When it comes to unfamiliar traditions and customs, it can be helpful to visualize them. Use the space below to draw the elements of the covenant described in this passage and the ritual of God walking between the animals. (Don't worry, stick figures are fine.)

2 What was the "detail" that made this particular ceremony so unusual? Notice that Abraham did not walk down the middle of the animals, which would have signaled that he was agreeing to his side of the deal. Rather, God put Abraham into a deep sleep and then alone walked between the pieces. Given this, what was God saying about this covenant?

APPLICATION

3 God provided this visual demonstration of his covenant to assure Abraham that he had not forgotten his promises. What are some of the ways that you have seen God remind you of his promises to you? How easy or difficult is it for you to believe his assurances?

4 What are some of the unconditional covenants that God has made with his people today?

5 What has learning about covenants in the Old Testament taught you about your relationship with God?

PRAYER

Father, you are the keeper of covenants. Even when I stray, you uphold your end of the bargain. You never leave me. You never forsake me. Thank you for this promise and thank you for the New Covenant that I have through Jesus. In his name, I pray. Amen.

WHO IS
LIKE YOU,
LORD GOD
ALMIGHTY?

PSALM 89:8

STUDY 3 | A Different Kind of God

We like to think we would do *anything* that God called us to do. Move to a faraway land like Abraham? Doable. Build a big boat like Noah? Okay. Bathe seven times in a muddy river? Gross . . . but sure. Yet if we're honest, there are limits to our faithfulness. There are tasks we just wouldn't do. Chief among them? Sacrificing our own child.

Yet this is what God instructed Abraham to do. "God said, 'Take your son, your only son, whom you love—Isaac—and go to the region of Moriah. Sacrifice him there as a burnt offering on a mountain I will show you" (Genesis 22:2). The story is disturbing. God wanted Abraham to sacrifice the son whom he had promised to provide? Most of us would not be able to carry our child up to the altar, much less go through with the actual sacrifice. If this story is simply a way to test Abraham, it seems cruel.

This is one of those stories in the Bible that makes more sense if you understand some cultural context. In the ancient world, child sacrifice was not uncommon. The fertility god of tribes and cultures in the ancient Near East often required a portion of what had been produced—whether that was grain, animals, or children—to be sacrificed.[10] Child sacrifice was particularly done in the name of Molech, a god of the Ammonites. So Abraham would not have been as surprised at the request as we are today.

Still, God had a bigger plan. Instead of requiring Abraham to sacrifice Isaac, he provided a ram to be sacrificed. God was making a statement: Human sacrifice was not required in order to be in a relationship with him and to continue receiving his blessings. Hebrew law would later forbid such child sacrifice (see Leviticus 18:21; 20:3; Deuteronomy 12:30–31; 18:10).

God was distinguishing himself from other gods—something crucial for him to do in a polytheistic world that shared beliefs, rituals, and deities. Abraham and his people would be set apart. This God came near to his people. He would be in an unconditional covenant relationship with them. He promised to bless and watch over them.

This is how we've always understood the God of the Bible. However, it's important to understand that for Abraham and those in his world, the idea of worshiping one God, much less a God who cared about and loved them, was a major religious and cultural shift. It is one that set a trajectory toward the birth of Christ—God in flesh, dwelling among us.

SCRIPTURE: Genesis 22:1–18

OBSERVATION

1 How did Abraham respond to God's instruction to sacrifice Isaac? What in the story indicates that he was fully prepared to go through with it?

2 How does knowing about the culture of Abraham's day impact how you see this story? What point was God making when he provided a ram in place of Isaac?

3 The apostle Paul wrote that God "did not spare his own Son, but gave him up for us all" (Romans 8:32). What was God willing to do that he did not require even of Abraham? What does this say about the length to which he went to free people everywhere from their sins?

APPLICATION

4 Think of a time when you felt "tested" by God. How did this period of testing affect your relationship with him? What was the outcome of that time of testing?

How this period of testing affected your relationship with God:

What the outcome was of this time of testing:

5 God told his people, "Apart from me there is no God" (Isaiah 44:6). Why was it important for the Israelites to know that Yahweh was not like the gods of the tribes and nations around them? Why is this same truth important for you today?

PRAYER

God, you are the one, true, and only God. I confess that sometimes I worship others gods in my life—like wealth and success—but I know that you are the only one worthy of my worship. Remind me of that truth today so I can stay focused on you. In your name, I pray. Amen.

CONNECT AND DISCUSS

Connect with a fellow group member and discuss some of the key insights from this session. Use any of the following prompts to help guide your discussion.

1. Of all the covenants you learned about during this session, which one stands out the most to you? Why that covenant?

2. What is something new that you learned about Creation and about Adam and Eve? How does this affect or change the way you view these early stories of the Bible?

3. How was the historical, cultural, or biblical context helpful to you in this week's session?

4. What common themes are you seeing in the stories of Adam and Eve and the patriarchs?

CATCH UP AND READ AHEAD

Use this time to go back and complete any of the study and reflection questions from previous days that you weren't able to finish. Make a note below of any revelations you've had and reflect on any growth or personal insights you've gained.

Read chapters 11–16 in *The Bible, Simplified* before the next group gathering. Use the space below to make note of anything in those chapters that stands out to you, inspires you, or encourages you.

Schedule | Week 3

BEFORE GROUP MEETING	Read chapters 11–16 in *The Bible, Simplified* Read the Welcome section (page 46)
GROUP MEETING	Discuss the Connect questions Watch the video teaching for session 3 Discuss the questions that follow as a group Do the closing exercise and pray (pages 46–50)
STUDY 1	Complete the personal study (pages 53–55)
STUDY 2	Complete the personal study (pages 57–59)
STUDY 3	Complete the personal study (pages 61–63)
CONNECT AND DISCUSS	Connect with one or two group members Discuss the follow-up questions (page 64)
CATCH UP AND READ AHEAD (before week 4 group meeting)	Read chapters 17–23 in *The Bible, Simplified* Complete any unfinished studies (page 65)

SESSION THREE

Building a Nation

Israel is on a roller coaster. Things are good, then things are bad, then things are okay, and then they crash. And it's always when they try to do things on their own that they crash the hardest.

Welcome [READ ON YOUR OWN]

You've likely heard it said that "Rome wasn't built in a day." This was certainly true for the nation of Israel. Building a nation takes time, strategy, victory, defeat, and more victory—all of which are part of Israel's story. But unlike Rome, Israel built their nation under the direction and protection of God, who had a plan for his people.

We see this plan in action when Joseph, a son of Jacob, is sold into slavery in Egypt. God enables Joseph to rise in power, with the result that his family is saved from a famine and moves to the land. This leads to the Israelites' enslavement in Egypt, their deliverance through Moses, and ultimately, their conquest of Canaan—a land God had promised to Abraham's descendants. The story of God's people is full of ups and downs: following God's way, forgetting God's way, turning from him, and then crying out to him.

You can likely relate. While you aren't building a nation, you are building a life. One that perhaps, like the Israelites, you dedicated to God and then began dedicating to . . . fill in the blank. *A job. Money. Success. Security. Dreams. Ambitions.* How many mornings do you wake up intending to please the Lord but by the end of the day your focus has shifted? You've made promises and you've broken them. But the good news, according to God's Word, is that this doesn't disqualify you from being part of God's people.

The Israelites had a hard time following God when they were a small tribe. Now they are trying to form a nation. God leads them out of Egypt and makes a covenant with them, but they break it. They finally enter the promised land, but they squander it. They ask for God for a king, but then pick one themselves. The Israelites' faithfulness to *God* comes and goes. Yet God's faithfulness to *them* remains the same. As Paul would later write, "If we are faithless, he remains faithful" (2 Timothy 2:13).

Connect [10 MINUTES]

Get this session started by choosing one or both of the following questions to discuss together as a group:

- What is something that spoke to you in last week's personal study that you would like to share with the group?

— *or* —

- When is a time you experienced God being faithful to you even though you were not faithful to him?

Watch [25 MINUTES]

Now watch the video for this session. Below is an outline of the key points covered during the teaching. Record any key concepts that stand out to you.

OUTLINE

I. How did the Israelites end up enslaved in Egypt?

A. Joseph's brothers sold him into slavery in Egypt, but he eventually rose to become Pharaoh's right-hand man.

B. Joseph's family moved to Egypt and were given land in Goshen.

C. The Israelites grew as a people group over the next four hundred years. A new Pharaoh arose who saw them as a threat and enslaved them.

II. How did God deliver his people from Egypt?

A. Pharaoh commanded all Israelite boys be drowned in the Nile River. But Moses (described as *tov)* was rescued by Pharaoh's daughter.

B. Moses was raised in Egyptian culture. He killed an Egyptian for beating an Israelite and fled to Midian, where he lived for the next forty years.

C. God met Moses in a burning bush and called him to deliver the Israelites. God sent a series of plagues to convince Pharaoh to let his people go.

D. God parted the Red Sea for the Israelites and established a new covenant with them through his law. The Israelites then built the tabernacle.

III. How did the Israelites enter into the promised land?

A. The Israelites feared the inhabitants of the promised land and refused to enter it. They spent the next forty years wandering in the desert.

B. The people were allowed to enter the promised land under Joshua. They conquered most of Canaan and divided the land among the twelve tribes.

C. The Israelites began to mix worship of Yahweh with worship of Baal.

D. This led to a downward spiral: The Israelites fell away from God and cried out to him, God delivered them (through judges), and then they sinned again. This cycle was repeated over and over.

IV. How did the Israelites eventually get a king?

A. The last judge of Israel was Samuel. He was also a prophet, and God used him to speak his words to the people of Israel.

B. The people wanted a king to lead them. God ultimately agreed and allowed *them* to choose a man named Saul. He looked strong like a king should.

C. Saul started off great, but pride and power were his downfall. God rejected him when he made his own decisions without Samuel and without God.

NOTES

EXODUS
CONQUEST
UNITED KINGDOM
Slavery (Egypt)
Passover
Mount Sinai
Promised Land
Judges
Monarchy (Saul)

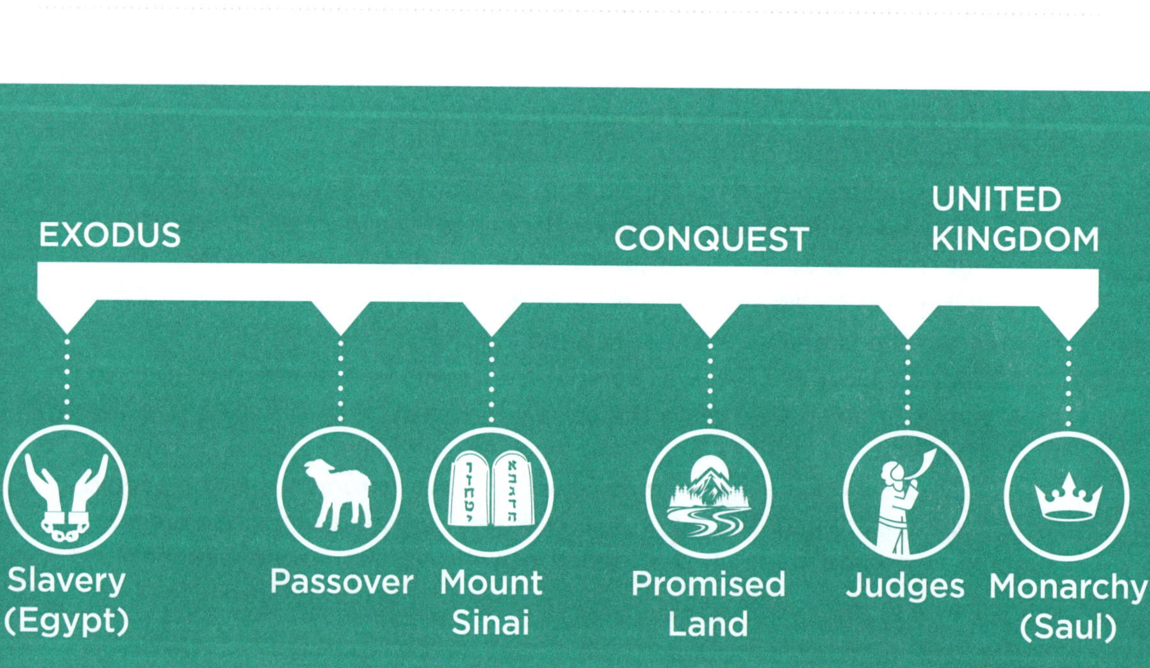

Discuss [35 MINUTES]

Discuss what you just watched by answering the following questions.

1. Ask someone to read Genesis 50:15–21. The story of Joseph is filled with ups and downs. Ultimately, God orchestrated events so he became second in command to Pharaoh. How does Joseph summarize the purpose of all that had happened to him? What does this say about how God works behind the scenes in our lives?

2. Ask someone to read aloud Exodus 1:6–11. At the end of Genesis, Joseph held one of the most powerful positions in the ancient world. By the beginning of Exodus, much has changed. What happened to the Israelites between Genesis and Exodus? Why do you think Pharaoh felt it necessary to take these steps against them?

3. Ask someone to read Judges 21:25. Joshua led the Israelites to conquer the promised land. Once there, they struggled to build a nation. Much of the problem was due to the fact that the people chose to mix worship of Yahweh with the worship of the gods in the nations around them. What does this verse say was the dire situation at that time? What future event does this verse look forward to?

4. Ask someone to read 1 Samuel 3:1–10 and 19–21. God raised up judges to rescue the Israelites when they fell into sin and then cried out to him for deliverance. Samuel was the last judge of Israel—but there was something else special about him. How did God reveal himself to Samuel? Why did Israel need a *prophet*?

5. Have someone read 1 Samuel 8:4–9. Who were the Israelites rejecting? How are we often like the Israelites—following other leaders before God?

Respond [10 MINUTES]

The book of 1 Samuel opens with a story about a woman named Hannah, who was unable to have children until God opened her womb. In her gratitude, she committed her son, Samuel, to the Lord. She prayed a prayer of thanksgiving after bringing Samuel to Eli, where he would be taught in the ways of God. Read the following passage and answer the questions below.

> [2] "There is no one holy like the LORD; there is no one besides you. . . . [3] Do not keep talking so proudly or let your mouth speak such arrogance, for the LORD is a God who knows, and by him deeds are weighed. [4] The bows of the warriors are broken, but those who stumbled are armed with strength. [5] Those who were full hire themselves out for food, but those who were hungry are hungry no more."
>
> **1 SAMUEL 2:2–5**

What are some of the ways you saw in this session that the Lord humbled those who thought they were mighty? How did God "weigh" his people's deeds?

What does Hannah's prayer say about her faith and what she understood about God?

Pray [10 MINUTES]

End your time in prayer. Thank God for the leadership he has placed over your life, your city, and your nation. Thank him for delivering you from sin in the same way he delivered the Israelites from slavery. Pray that you would always remember who the true king is and whom you serve. Ask for discernment to hear his voice and always obey his commands.

SESSION THREE

PERSONAL STUDY

Building a nation isn't easy, especially when that nation is meant to be set apart from all the rest. The God of Israel was holy, and his people were meant to be holy. As God said to Abraham, "All peoples on earth will be blessed through you" (Genesis 12:3). This was God's intention—for his people to bless the other nations by pointing them to the one true God. Sometimes, they were faithful to this mission. More often, they just tried to blend in and be like the other nations. As you will see in this week's personal studies, the Israelites struggled to grow into the people God wanted them to be—and this had disastrous consequences for them. As you work through the exercises, write down your responses, as you will be given time to share your insights at the start of the next session if you are doing this study with others. If you are reading *The Bible, Simplified* alongside this study, first review chapters 11–16 in the book.

ISRAEL DURING THE JUDGES

STUDY 1 | God's Own Name

Names are important. Soon-to-be parents agonize over what to name their child. They search lists of baby names to find a strong name, or a meaningful name, or a beautiful name. They avoid names that have negative associations and memories for them.

Names are also important in the Bible. Often, they are symbolic and represent who the person was or the call that was on the person's life. Knowing the meaning behind a name in the Bible can help us better understand a character or his or her circumstances. And no name in Scripture is more important—or more in need of understanding—than the name of God.

We often refer to our divine creator as *God*. Or maybe *the Lord* at times. Or *Savior*, when referring to his Son. But for the ancient Israelites, the name of God was so sacred they didn't even speak it out loud. This name was also different from the ones we use for God: YHWH. Ancient Hebrew had no written vowels, so it is not known how this would have been pronounced (or even if it was spoken out loud). In English, it is often rendered *Yahweh* or, in some of the older translations, by its Latinized form, *Jehovah*.

This name for God is introduced right after the story of Moses and the burning bush in the book of Exodus. Moses asks, "Suppose I go to the Israelites and say to them, 'The God of your fathers has sent me to you,' and they ask me, 'What is his name?' Then what shall I tell them?" (3:13). God replies, "I AM WHO I AM. This is what you are to say to the Israelites: 'I AM has sent me to you'" (verse 14). God then instructs Moses, "Say to the Israelites, 'The LORD, the God of your fathers—the God of Abraham, the God of Isaac and the God of Jacob—has sent me to you'" (verse 15). The word that appears in small caps as *Lord* in that verse is Yahweh (YHWH).

Yahweh signifies a God who has always been—thus the declaration "I AM"—and who always will be. The name evokes a God who is ever-present and ever-active in his people's lives. The Israelites, who felt forgotten by God during this time of Egyptian enslavement, needed this reminder. We need it too. It's easy to feel as if God has forgotten us and no longer works in our lives like he did in the Bible, showing up in burning bushes, casting plagues, thundering from mountaintops, and parting seas.

But the Yahweh of the Israelites is the same Yahweh of today. He is I *am*, not I *was*. Just as he answered the Israelites when they cried out him, so he will answer us.

SCRIPTURE: Matthew 1:18–24

OBSERVATION

1. The name given in Scripture to the Son of God also carries great meaning. *Jesus* is the Greek form of the name *Joshua*, which can mean either "Yahweh is salvation" or "Yahweh saves." How is this name appropriate, given what the angel says he will do (see verse 21)?

2. The name *Immanuel* literally means "God with us" (see verse 23). It is closer to a title for Jesus than an actual name. What does this particular name say about God's ongoing mission in the world? What was God reaffirming to his people through this name?

APPLICATION

3. The name the angel used for Jesus—*Immanuel*—was a reassurance that God had not forgotten his people. In what area of your life do you need this same reassurance today? Why do you especially need this reassurance?

4 The name *I Am* reveals that God is ever-present and unchanging. The name *Jesus* reveals that he is your salvation. The name *Immanuel* reveals that he is always with you. How can these names of God encourage you the next time you feel alone or forgotten by him?

5 List a few of the significant names in your family. These could be names that are meaningful in and of themselves or names of people who evoke reverence and respect in your family.

NAME	Why is this name significant?

PRAYER

Jesus, your name is the one "that is above every name" (Philippians 2:9). Your name has power to save. Your name reminds me that I am never forsaken or alone. Your name is a comfort in times of despair. Remind me of your name today. May I cling to it when I have nothing else. Thank you for the hope your name gives me. Amen.

MOST
HOLY
PLACE

STUDY 2 | The Most Holy Place

One of the first orders of business for Israel after they were led out of Egypt was to build the tabernacle. This structure was a portable tent where God would dwell among his people. As the Lord said to Moses, "Make this tabernacle and all its furnishings exactly like the pattern I will show you" (Exodus 25:9).

These instructions are provided in great detail in Exodus 25–31. However, for the sake of this study, we will focus on just one set of instructions: "Make a curtain of blue, purple and scarlet yarn and finely twisted linen, with cherubim woven into it by a skilled worker. Hang it with gold hooks on four posts of acacia wood overlaid with gold and standing on four silver bases. Hang the curtain from the clasps and place the ark of the covenant law behind the curtain. The curtain will separate the Holy Place from the Most Holy Place. Put the atonement cover on the ark of the covenant law in the Most Holy Place" (Exodus 26:31–34).

God here is instructing the people to hang a curtain in the tabernacle to separate the *Holy Place* from the *Most Holy Place*. Remember that the term *holy* means "set apart." Both the Holy Place and the Most Holy Place would be set apart from any other place on earth by the fact that God's presence would dwell there. The Holy Place was where the priest would enter. The Most Holy Place, also known as the Holy of Holies, was where the presence of God would reside. It is also where the Ark of the Covenant was housed. God had told Moses, "No one may see me and live" (Exodus 33:20)—thus the need for a curtain to separate the two areas.

Only the high priest could go into the Most Holy Place, and he could only do so once a year on the Day of Atonement—a day when Israel's sins were forgiven. The tabernacle was thus incredibly significant to the nation. Israel went from being enslaved in Egypt, wondering where God was and if he had forgotten them, to being a free people with God dwelling among them. It was yet another promise of *I Am*—God's nearness.

It's also an important promise for us today. As one scholar noted, "The tabernacle overturns a popular misconception in Christianity that God's holiness prevents him from being near human sin. On the contrary, God makes it his purpose to live among his people, and he draws nearer and nearer throughout human history."[11] Though we may not worship in tabernacles today, the temple of God is still very much alive, and his presence is still near.

SCRIPTURE: Matthew 27:45–51; 1 Corinthians 3:16–17; Hebrews 9:1–15

OBSERVATION

1. Just as there was a curtain separating the Holy Place from the Most Holy Place during the time of Moses, so there was a curtain that separated those places in the temple during the time of Christ. What happened to that curtain at Jesus' death? What did that event signify for God's people from that time forward?

2. Where does Paul say in 1 Corinthians 3:16–17 that the temple now resides? What are the implications of this when it comes to living a holy life?

3. The author of Hebrews compares and contrasts what is was like for God's people before the veil was torn and what it is like for them now. Look up each of the following passages in Hebrews 9:1–15 and write down what was true *before* this event and what was true *after*.

BEFORE	**AFTER**
verses 2–3:	verse 11:
verses 6–7:	verse 12:
verse 9:	verse 14:
verse 1:	verse 15:

APPLICATION

4 The tabernacle was a place of worship for the Israelites that signified God's presence among them.

Why are these types of places likewise important to your faith?

What is a place like the tabernacle where you go to spend time with God and experience his presence?

5 How do you feel about the idea of God living inside of you—of God's own Spirit dwelling in your midst? How have you experienced his presence inside of you?

PRAYER

Dear God, you have made your home in my heart, and your dwelling place is now inside of me. I don't always feel worthy of this. I don't always want this! I sometimes want to be far from you so I can do what I please rather than what pleases you. Forgive me when I stray. Thank you that no matter how far I go, you are always with me. In Jesus' name, I pray. Amen.

God had one goal

TO KEEP HIS PEOPLE HOLY

STUDY 3 | Israel's Neighbors

A major theme in the Old Testament is that God had called the Israelites to be a monotheistic people in a polytheistic world. The ancient world was full of polytheistic tribes and cultures—people who worshiped many gods rather than the one true God.

When you are the minority religion in the land, it's easy to get swept up in the current of who everybody else is worshiping. This is why God, time and again, warned his people about the dangers of choosing to live side by side with these cultures. They had "man-made gods of wood and stone" (Deuteronomy 4:28)—gods with a physical presence. This was alluring to a people whose God could not be seen.

Sadly, the history of the Israelite people reveals that they never completely separated themselves from the societies around them. Great gains were made under the leadership of Joshua. Many foreign nations *were* conquered and dispersed from the promised land. However, after his death, the situation took a turn for the worse:

> [1] The angel of the LORD went up from Gilgal to Bokim and said, "I brought you up out of Egypt and led you into the land I swore to give to your ancestors. I said, 'I will never break my covenant with you, [2] and you shall not make a covenant with the people of this land, but you shall break down their altars.' Yet you have disobeyed me. Why have you done this? [3] And I have also said, 'I will not drive them out before you; they will become traps for you, and their gods will become snares to you'" (Judges 2:1–3).

God had one goal: to keep his people holy. The Israelites' failure to obey him in this regard would have consequences for their future. As God said, "I will no longer drive out before them any of the nations Joshua left when he died. I will use them to test Israel and see whether they will keep the way of the LORD" (verses 21–22). The rest of Judges is one sad tale after another of how the people continued to compromise by worshiping the gods of their neighbors instead of Yahweh.

God knew his people's hearts. He wanted to protect them from themselves. Joshua had said, "Choose for yourselves this day whom you will serve" (Joshua 24:15). God wanted them to choose to worship *him*, but the people of Israel repeatedly made the wrong choice. Their story serves as a warning to us today. Will we choose to follow the "idols" of this world? Or will we choose to dedicate our hearts to serving Yahweh?

SCRIPTURE: Numbers 25:1–3; Judges 6:25–32; 1 Samuel 7:3–4

OBSERVATION

1. God's message to the Israelites in Deuteronomy 20:16–18 came as they prepared to enter into the promised land. Why did God want them to "completely destroy" these groups? What are some of the "detestable things" these groups did in worshiping their gods?

2. Gideon's story in Judges 6 is a vivid example of how the Israelites were engaging in the worship of foreign gods. What did God command Gideon to do? What did Joash, Gideon's father, understand about the foreign gods that were in Israel?

3. According to 1 Samuel 7:3–4, what was the situation in Israel at the time of Samuel? What does this verse say about the people's spiritual state?

APPLICATION

4. Have you ever been influenced by a group that you knew was not doing the right thing? If so, what did God teach you through that experience?

5 It is easy to fault the Israelites for falling into idol worship, yet we still allow idols in our world today to vie for our attention, time, and worship. Consider some of the following common idols in our society. How much of a pull would you say these have on your life?

IDOL	**How much pull does this have on you?**
Money (security in wealth)	
Comfort (security in the good things in life)	
Power (security in getting your way)	
Status (security in being esteemed by all)	
Success (security in "being someone")	

PRAYER

God, you have called me to lead a holy life in a world that is generally anything but holy. Help me to keep my eyes focused on you and not be tempted to follow after the idols of this world. Help me to be a person who always points others toward your glory. In your name, I pray. Amen.

CONNECT AND DISCUSS

Connect with a fellow group member and discuss some of the key insights from this session. Use any of the following prompts to help guide your discussion.

1. Why was Moses an unlikely person to lead the Israelites out of slavery in Egypt? What does this reveal about the kind of people God uses?

2. What does God's name reveal about him? Why did he want his people to remember this name "from generation to generation" (Exodus 3:15)?

3. In what ways were the Israelites to be different from the cultures around them? How successful were they in remaining different?

4. Why did the people ultimately ask God to give them a king? What does this reveal about just how similar they had become to other nations?

CATCH UP AND READ AHEAD

Use this time to go back and complete any of the study and reflection questions from previous days that you weren't able to finish. Make a note below of any revelations you've had and reflect on any growth or personal insights you've gained.

Read chapters 17–23 in *The Bible, Simplified* before the next group gathering. Use the space below to make note of anything in those chapters that stands out to you, inspires you, or encourages you.

Schedule | Week 4

BEFORE GROUP MEETING	Read chapters 17–23 in *The Bible, Simplified* Read the Welcome section (page 68)
GROUP MEETING	Discuss the Connect questions Watch the video teaching for session 4 Discuss the questions that follow as a group Do the closing exercise and pray (pages 68–72)
STUDY 1	Complete the personal study (pages 75–77)
STUDY 2	Complete the personal study (pages 79–81)
STUDY 3	Complete the personal study (pages 83–85)
CONNECT AND DISCUSS	Connect with one or two group members Discuss the follow-up questions (page 86)
CATCH UP AND READ AHEAD (before week 5 group meeting)	Read chapters 24–32 in *The Bible, Simplified* Complete any unfinished studies (page 87)

SESSION FOUR

Downfall of a Nation

The people of Israel were ruled by kings. However, this would lead to their downfall, as king after king led them into the worship of foreign gods. Ultimately, God allowed them to be conquered by other nations and taken into exile. In time, the people were allowed to return to their land—and this time they decided to rebuild with God as the foundation.

Welcome [READ ON YOUR OWN]

God had chosen the Israelites "out of all the peoples on the face of the earth to be his people, his treasured possession" (Deuteronomy 7:6). He wanted them to acknowledge that *he* was their true king and judge. Yet the people of Israel were not content with this arrangement. "We want a king over us," they cried. "Then we will be like all the other nations, with a king to lead us and to go out before us and fight our battles" (1 Samuel 8:19–20).

The Lord understood the Israelites were rejecting him as king, but in his mercy, he allowed them to choose a human to reign over them. As you saw in the last session, *their* choice, Saul, was a failure. However, *God's* choice for the next king, David, would be a godly man who would move the nation forward. Israel would experience an unparalleled time of prosperity and peace during both David's reign and that of his son Solomon.

Sadly, as you will explore in this session, as quickly as Israel rose, it just as quickly fell. A human monarchy did not lead to the unity and strength the people had hoped for but rather to division and weakness. It didn't take long for the kings to slowly but surely lead the people away from the worship of Yahweh. This, in turn, would lead to exile.

Perhaps you can see yourself in Israel's story. You've also had plans that didn't work out the way you expected. You've also spent years building something—a marriage, a career, a business—only to witness it crumble. You also feel as if you are in exile. However, as you will also see in this session, God has given you the same promise of renewal and restoration that he gave to the Israelites. When he is your king, nothing is ever truly lost forever.

Connect [10 MINUTES]

Get this session started by choosing one or both of the following questions to discuss together as a group:

- What is something that spoke to you in last week's personal study that you would like to share with the group?

— *or* —

- When have you lost something in your life that you worked hard to build?

Watch [25 MINUTES]

Now watch the video for this session. Below is an outline of the key points covered during the teaching. Record any key concepts that stand out to you.

OUTLINE

I. What led to David becoming king and the Davidic Covenant?

A. God rejected Saul as king and sent Samuel to anoint his replacement.

B. David was anointed and, after Saul's death, eventually became king.

C. David established Jerusalem as the capital city and moved the Ark of the Covenant there. He wanted to build a temple to the Lord.

D. God promised to one day send a Messiah—a king through David's royal line—who would establish the Lord's eternal kingdom on earth.

II. What led to the division of Israel and the downfall of the two kingdoms?

A. David's son Solomon asked God for wisdom and built the temple.

B. Solomon married women from other cultures, which led to worship of Yahweh being mixed with foreign gods. This began Israel's downfall.

C. After Solomon's death, the ten northern tribes formed the kingdom of Israel and the two southern tribes formed the kingdom of Judah.

D. Assyria destroyed the northern kingdom in 722 BC. Babylon conquered the southern kingdom in 587 BC and took its people into exile.

III. What led to the exile and then to the people's return to the land?

A. God sent prophets to warn his people of their coming destruction and exile—punishment for worshiping false gods and committing acts of evil.

B. These prophets also told of a time when the people would return to Jerusalem and rebuild the temple. This happened after seventy years in exile.

C. King Cyrus of Persia defeated the Babylonians in 539 BC. He allowed the exiles to return home to Jerusalem—though many chose to stay in Persia.

IV. What happened after the Israelites returned to the land?

A. The exiles who returned were more focused on rebuilding their city than they were on rebuilding God's temple.

B. So God sent the prophet Ezra to restore God's covenant with his people. He then sent Nehemiah to help rebuild Jerusalem's walls to protect them from their enemies.

C. The prophets continued to speak of a Messiah who would restore God's kingdom. However, four hundred years of silence would pass before this promised Messiah came on the scene.

NOTES

UNITED KINGDOM
DIVIDED KINGDOM
EXILE
RETURN
Monarchy (David)
Capture Jerusalem
Kingdom Divides
Exile
Return
Walls Rebuilt

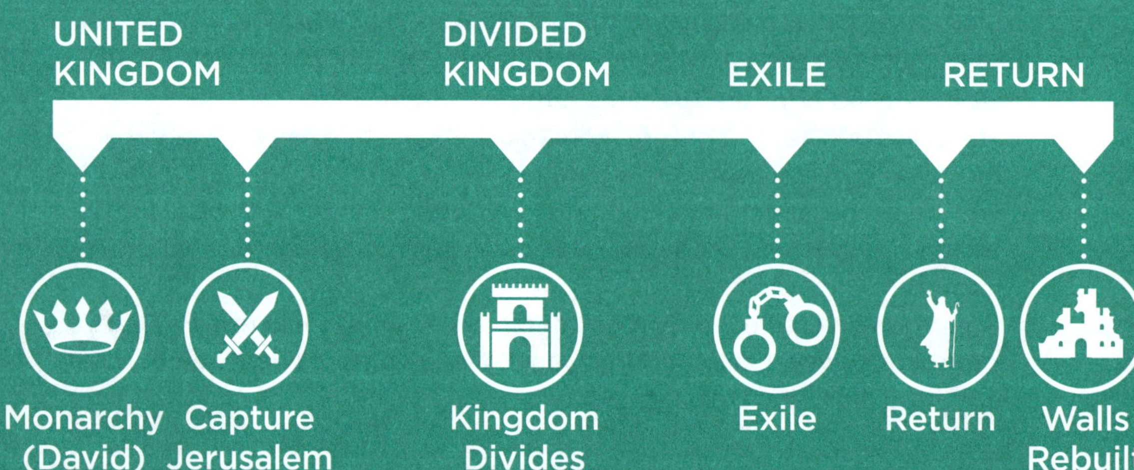

Discuss [35 MINUTES]

Discuss what you just watched by answering the following questions.

1. The people of Israel had faltered under King Saul, but they entered into a golden age of peace and prosperity under David. What was different about the selections of Saul and David? What was different about David's heart as compared to Saul's?

2. David and Solomon were similar in both positive and negative ways. How did their sins have an effect not only on them and the people directly involved but also on the nation? What does this reveal about what God expects in his leaders?

3. Ask someone to read aloud Jeremiah 25:4–11. What was God's complaint against the people of Judah? Why did he allow them to be taken into captivity?

4. Ask someone to read Psalm 44:13–19. What did the people come to understand during their seventy years of exile? How did God use the exile to return their hearts to him?

5. Have someone read Nehemiah 2:17–18. King Artaxerxes allowed Nehemiah to lead the effort in rebuilding Jerusalem's walls—and even gave him the resources to do so. What did rebuilding Jerusalem's walls symbolize for God's people? When has God likewise provided you with the guidance and resources to rebuild something that was broken in your life?

Respond [10 MINUTES]

The prophets in the Bible operated during the decline of Israel and Judah. They frequently rebuked the people for their past sins and told of what would happen if they continued in that sin. Yet they also often offered a message of hope from the Lord. It seems that with every prophecy about their downfall, there was a prophecy about God reestablishing his covenant with them. Read the following passage that reflects this truth and answer the questions below.

> 6 For to us a child is born, to us a son is given, and the government will be on his shoulders. And he will be called Wonderful Counselor, Mighty God, Everlasting Father, Prince of Peace. 7 Of the greatness of his government and peace there will be no end. He will reign on David's throne and over his kingdom, establishing and upholding it with justice and righteousness from that time on and forever.
>
> **ISAIAH 9:6–7**

The Israelites were familiar with the Davidic Covenant and were expecting the coming of a Messiah. What did Isaiah say this individual's "government" and "kingdom" would be like?

How do you think the people of Israel would have reacted to this affirmation that the Messiah was indeed coming? What, if anything, might have stood out to them from Isaiah's description?

Pray [10 MINUTES]

Close by praying together in your group. Thank God for being faithful to you even when you are not faithful to him. If you are in a season of exile, ask the Lord to be with you. If you are in a season of returning home, praise him for it. Ask him for wisdom and guidance as you rebuild the parts of your life that were once broken.

SESSION FOUR
PERSONAL STUDY

Israel under King David and Solomon became the envy of the other nations. But the good times did not last. After the nation broke apart into a northern and southern kingdom, a series of (mostly) ungodly kings plunged the people further into the worship of foreign gods. Ultimately, this led to the extinction of the northern kingdom and the exile of the people in the southern kingdom. In this personal study, you will learn more about God's instructions to those who survived in exile. You will also explore two other types of literature in the Old Testament: the books of poetry and the books of wisdom. As you work through the exercises, write down your responses to the questions, as you will be given a few minutes to share your insights at the start of the next session if you are doing this study with others. If you are reading *The Bible, Simplified* alongside this study, first review chapters 17–23 in the book.

THE UNITED KINGDOM

STUDY 1 | Poetry

A favorite book, poem, song, or TV show can be a great comfort during a difficult time. Perhaps you can recall a time you found yourself flipping through familiar pages or listening to soothing lyrics when life took a turn you didn't expect. This is one of the great powers of art. It can meet you where you are and—at least for a moment—give you a reprieve, a cathartic emotional release, or a promise of hope for the future.

This is how Psalms came to be. While the poems and songs that make up the book were composed over a span of at least five centuries—with the earliest (Psalm 90) believed to have been written by Moses—they began to be collected by the Jewish people during the Babylonian exile. Some of the psalms directly address the people's exile and express their honest emotions toward the Lord, like the psalm below:

> Awake, Lord! Why do you sleep?
>   Rouse yourself! Do not reject us forever (Psalm 44:23).

Others rebuke the people of Israel for turning from God:

> But they put God to the test
>   and rebelled against the Most High;
>   they did not keep his statutes (Psalm 78:56).

And others simply lament their being in a foreign land:

> By the rivers of Babylon we sat and wept
>   when we remembered Zion (Psalm 137:1).

During one of the darkest times in their history, the Israelites turned to poetry to help process their exile and their relationship with God. We can use the psalms to do the same. There is a psalm for every season. Psalms of lament when you're grieving. Psalms of praise when you feel thankful. Psalms of wisdom for when you need guidance.

David authored nearly half the psalms. His life was full of ups and downs, joy and grief, times of closeness with God and times of distance. His psalms provide a wealth of literature you can turn to when life is good, when life is hard, and when you need to be honest with God—further proof this text is as applicable today as it was back then.

SCRIPTURE: Psalm 23:1–6; 90:1–17; 127:1–5

OBSERVATION

1. Psalm 23, written by David, is a "thanksgiving psalm." Write down the imagery David uses in the first three verses to describe God's guidance.

> [1] The LORD is my ____________, I lack nothing.
> [2] He makes me lie down in ________ __________,
> he leads me beside ________ _________,
> [3] he ____________ my soul.
> He guides me along the ________ ________
> for his name's sake.

2. Psalm 90, which scholars believe to have been written by Moses, is a "communal lament." What is the overall tone of this psalm? Why does Moses ask God to "teach us to number our days" (verse 12)?

3. Psalm 127, written by Solomon, is a "wisdom psalm." Write down the imagery Solomon uses in the first verse to describe God's sovereignty.

> [1] Unless the LORD ________ the ________,
> the __________ labor in vain.
> Unless the LORD ________ over the city,
> the _________ stand _________ in vain.

APPLICATION

4 Is it easy or difficult for you to be honest about your emotions with God? Why?

5 How could reading the psalms help you process difficult seasons, feelings, and thoughts—even if those are difficult thoughts toward God?

Difficult seasons . . .

Difficult feelings . . .

Difficult thoughts . . .

PRAYER

Father, thank you for giving me the psalms. Thank you for allowing me to express my emotions, fears, and doubts. You do not shy away from this honesty but embrace it and meet me in the midst of it. Help me to continue being honest with you. In your name, amen.

WHY DO
GOOD
PEOPLE
SUFFER?

STUDY 2 | Wisdom

The word *wisdom* is used some 234 times in Scripture, depending on the translation.[12] The Old and New Testaments often instruct us to pursue wisdom, live wisely, and seek understanding. As Proverbs 3:13–14 says, "Blessed are those who find wisdom, those who gain understanding, for she is more profitable than silver and yields better returns than gold."

Proverbs is considered one of the "wisdom books"—a key literary genre in the Bible. In addition to Proverbs, other wisdom books include Ecclesiastes, Song of Songs, and Job. The book of Job is a particularly interesting story about a righteous man whom God allows to be tested by Satan. The tests are brutal and beg the question: *Why do good people suffer?*

Job's suffering became so great that he wished he were dead. His questions for God reflect his anguish: "Will you never look away from me, or let me alone even for an instant? If I have sinned, what have I done to you, you who see everything we do? Why have you made me your target? Have I become a burden to you? Why do you not pardon my offenses and forgive my sins? For I will soon lie down in the dust; you will search for me, but I will be no more" (Job 7:19–21).

We've all asked similar questions. We've wondered where God is and if he cares. But how often do we voice these questions to God or to others in our faith community? After all, questions like these can feel taboo in our churches and small groups. But the people in the Bible asked them often—and God wasn't afraid of them.

When you think about it, this only makes sense. After all, how can you have a relationship with someone if you never ask why that person does something? Or if you never have a conflict that you must work through together? Or if you never express any of your feelings to that individual? Questions bring people closer together. The same is true of our relationship with God.

We fear asking these questions because we don't want to be labeled a doubter or weak in our faith. But stories like Job prove that these questions are not *forbidden* but *welcome*. God meets us in our questions, and as our relationship with him grows, so does our wisdom.

SCRIPTURE: Job 1:13–19; 2:7–8; 38:4–11; 42:2–6

OBSERVATION

1 Write down all of Job's afflictions described in Job 1:13–19 and 2:7–8.

PASSAGE	AFFLICTION
1:13–15	
1:16	
1:17	
1:18–19	
2:7–8	

2 After everything is taken from Job, his friends come to visit him. Each one takes turns trying to provide an explanation for what had happened to Job. Then God himself visits. What does he say in Job 38:4–11? What point is God trying to make?

3 According to Job 42:2–6, what wisdom did Job glean from this experience?

APPLICATION

4 What are some of the profound afflictions that you have faced in your life? What questions did you have about God during those times of suffering?

5 How did the Lord meet you in your questions and suffering? What wisdom did you gain?

PRAYER

Father, you know all the afflictions I face today. You know my suffering. You have felt it first-hand. Please be with me as I endure these seasons of life. Help me not to forget who you are. Keep me close to you even as I question you. In Jesus' name, I pray. Amen.

LIVING
IN
EXILE

STUDY 3 | How to Live in Exile

So, what happened to the Israelites *while* they were in exile? Were they imprisoned? Were they suffering? Were they thriving? Did they conform to the ways of the Babylonians? Or did they maintain their religion and culture while in a foreign territory?

The stories of Daniel and Esther take place during the time of exile. Daniel, along with his three friends, was taken captive by Nebuchadnezzar II of Babylon. In exile, the men remained faithful to their Jewish dietary laws (see Daniel 1:8–16) and refused to worship a golden image of the king (see 3:1–30). Later, under the Persians, Daniel refused to worship anyone other than Yahweh (see 6:6–14). Esther was also an exile in Persia. She was willing to risk her life and go before King Xerxes to intercede on behalf of her people.

Daniel and Esther are examples of how some of the Jewish people were able to live *in* the culture without being assimilated *by* the culture. They remained true to God while still participating in the societies in which they found themselves. They didn't try to run away or withdraw but served God in the place where he had planted them.

The Lord had actually given his people instructions for how to live in exile, saying to them, "Build houses and settle down; plant gardens and eat what they produce. Marry and have sons and daughters; find wives for your sons and give your daughters in marriage, so that they too may have sons and daughters. Increase in number there; do not decrease. Also, seek the peace and prosperity of the city to which I have carried you into exile" (Jeremiah 29:5–7).

Build communities, have children, seek peace and prosperity. Notice that God didn't tell them to *keep their distance from the Babylonians, pitch their tents on the city's border,* or *be ready to leave at a moment's notice*. He wanted them to settle in as if the land was their home. He wanted them to seek peace and prosperity for themselves and those around them.

When you find yourself in a season of exile because of suffering, depression, abandonment, or something else, you might be tempted to spend your time watching the clock. *I don't belong here. And I want to get out of here. So I'll just bide my time until this difficulty is done.* But God's words to the Jewish exiles suggest you should do otherwise. *Settle in where you are. Be a blessing to those around you. Be patient and kind.*

SCRIPTURE: Daniel 6:6–14; Esther 4:4–16; Jeremiah 29:10–14

OBSERVATION

1. Daniel had so distinguished himself in Persia that many were jealous of him.

   How did Daniel demonstrate he had remained faithful to God in exile?

   What does King Darius's reaction to his fate reveal about how Daniel had "bloomed" where God had planted him?

2. How did Esther reveal that she had also remained true to her people and her God? How did she use the position God had given her to intercede for her race?

3. God assured his people in Jeremiah 29:10–14 that the exile would not last forever. Write down every "I will" statement God makes in this passage.

   verse 10: I will ______________________________

   verse 12: I will ______________________________

   verse 14: I will be ______________________________

verse 14: and will ____

verse 14: I will ____

verse 14: and will ____

APPLICATION

4 When has God allowed you to be in a season of exile? How did you respond to being there?

5 How is God using you for his kingdom right now—in whatever place that he has planted you?

PRAYER

God, even in times of exile you are with me. I confess that I often want to escape, but you have called me to be still. Help me be patient as I wait for my deliverance. Show me how I can be a blessing to those around me. I trust in your perfect timing. In Jesus' name, amen.

CONNECT AND DISCUSS

Connect with a fellow group member and discuss some of the key insights from this session. Use any of the following prompts to help guide your discussion.

1. Of the types of biblical literature discussed—prophecy, poetry, and wisdom—which one are you the most interested in reading? Why?

2. Which season of Israel's story most resonates with you: the golden era under King David, the exile in Babylon, or the rebuilding of Jerusalem? Why that particular season?

3. Why was it so difficult for the Israelites to remain separate from the cultures around them? Why it is often so difficult for us today?

4. What common themes do you see in the story of Israel as a nation?

CATCH UP AND READ AHEAD

Use this time to go back and complete any of the study and reflection questions from previous days that you weren't able to finish. Make a note below of any revelations you've had and reflect on any growth or personal insights you've gained.

Read chapters 24–32 in *The Bible, Simplified* before the next group gathering. Use the space below to make note of anything in those chapters that stands out to you, inspires you, or encourages you.

Schedule | Week 5

BEFORE GROUP MEETING	Read chapters 24–32 in *The Bible, Simplified* Read the Welcome section (page 90)
GROUP MEETING	Discuss the Connect questions Watch the video teaching for session 5 Discuss the questions that follow as a group Do the closing exercise and pray (pages 90–94)
STUDY 1	Complete the personal study (pages 97–99)
STUDY 2	Complete the pesonal study (pages 101–103)
STUDY 3	Complete the personal study (pages 105–107)
CONNECT AND DISCUSS	Connect with one or two group members Discuss the follow-up questions (page 108)
CATCH UP AND READ AHEAD (before week 6 group meeting)	Read chapters 33–36 in *The Bible, Simplified* Complete any unfinished studies (page 109)

SESSION FIVE

Jesus, the Messiah

God sent his Son, Jesus, to end the sacrificial system and usher in a new age of humanity. He took the punishment for our sins and gave us the gift of life. If we accept his sacrifice as our own, we become part of a new family that can now be in communion with God.

Welcome [READ ON YOUR OWN]

Up to this point, you've spent a lot of time in the Old Testament—perhaps more than you ever have in the past! If you are like many Christians, you likely tend to focus on the New Testament. However, as you've discovered, Jesus is not only present in the *New* Testament but also in the *Old* Testament. In truth, every part of the ancient Hebrew Bible points to the event you will learn about today: the coming of the Messiah.

Immediately after the Fall, God announced that a descendant of Eve would come to "crush [the enemy's] head" (Genesis 3:15). The Lord provided further details about this coming Messiah through the psalmists and the prophets. Jesus, born some four hundred years after the prophet Malachi penned the last words of the Old Testament, would be this Messiah and Savior of the world.

When he arrived, he announced God's kingdom had arrived. Many dismissed him. The Jewish people were expecting the Messiah to be a political ruler who would free them from Rome. Yet some did become his followers, and many witnessed his miracles. Rumblings and murmurs soon began to spread that Jesus *could* be the promised Messiah. This brought hope to many, while for others—including the Pharisees, Sadducees, and Roman leaders—it felt threatening. These groups tried to eradicate Jesus and his message. Yet, try as they might, they could not thwart God's plan to redeem humanity through the sacrifice of his Son. The Lord would follow through on it.

In the beginning, God's plan was to establish his kingdom on earth. This plan went awry when Adam and Eve sinned. But God never gave up on us nor on the idea that heaven and earth could one day coexist, with him as our king and us as his people.

Connect [10 MINUTES]

Get this session started by choosing one or both of the following questions to discuss together as a group:

- What is something that spoke to you in last week's personal study that you would like to share with the group?

— *or* —

- What is one of the greatest kingdoms that has existed on earth? What do you know about that kingdom's particular legacy?

Watch [25 MINUTES]

Now watch the video for this session. Below is an outline of the key points covered during the teaching. Record any key concepts that stand out to you.

OUTLINE

I. What happened during the "four hundred years of silence"?

A. Four hundred years passed between the last Old Testament prophet and the birth of the Messiah. Yet God was working behind the scenes.

B. Alexander the Great rose to power, which spread Greek (Hellenistic) culture into Jerusalem. Jewish persecution led to the Maccabean revolt.

C. Internal fighting led to the Romans being invited in to restore peace. God used these events to prepare the world for the spread of the gospel.

D. Finally, John the Baptist, who would pave the way for Jesus, was born.

II. How did the Messiah enter the world and begin his ministry?

A. A woman named Mary is told by an angel that she will give birth to the Messiah. Her fiancé, Joseph, has a dream that affirms the baby is from God.

B. John the Baptist—the last Old Testament prophet—appears. He preaches, "Repent, for the kingdom of heaven has come near" (Matthew 3:2).

C. Jesus shows up as John is baptizing people. When Jesus is baptized, the spirit of God descends on him, declaring him to be the Son of God.

D. God was beginning the process of merging heaven and earth.

III. What took place during Jesus' ministry on earth?

A. Jesus is taken into the wilderness to be tempted by the devil.

B. Jesus emerges preaching a message of repentance like John but adds, "The kingdom of God is in your midst" (Luke 17:21).

C. Jesus chooses twelve disciples (a symbolic number) to study under him as their rabbi. They spread his message of God's kingdom—the "good news."

IV. What led to Jesus' death and resurrection?

A. Tensions rise between Jesus and the religious elite—primarily the Pharisees and Sadducees—who expected the Messiah to conquer the physical world.

B. Jesus goes to Jerusalem for the Passover. In Gethsemane, he wrestles with the fact that he—though sinless—will take on humanity's sins.

C. The Jewish leaders arrange for Jesus to be arrested. He is tried, convicted, beaten, and mocked. He dies on the cross at three o'clock in the afternoon.

D. Three days later, Jesus rises, defeating death and hell. Jesus—sinless and spotless—becomes the perfect sacrifice for humanity's sins.

NOTES

THE MESSIAH
JESUS' MINISTRY
Birth
Baptism & Temptation
Calling Disciples
Teaching & Miracles
Arrest & Trials
Death
Empty Tomb

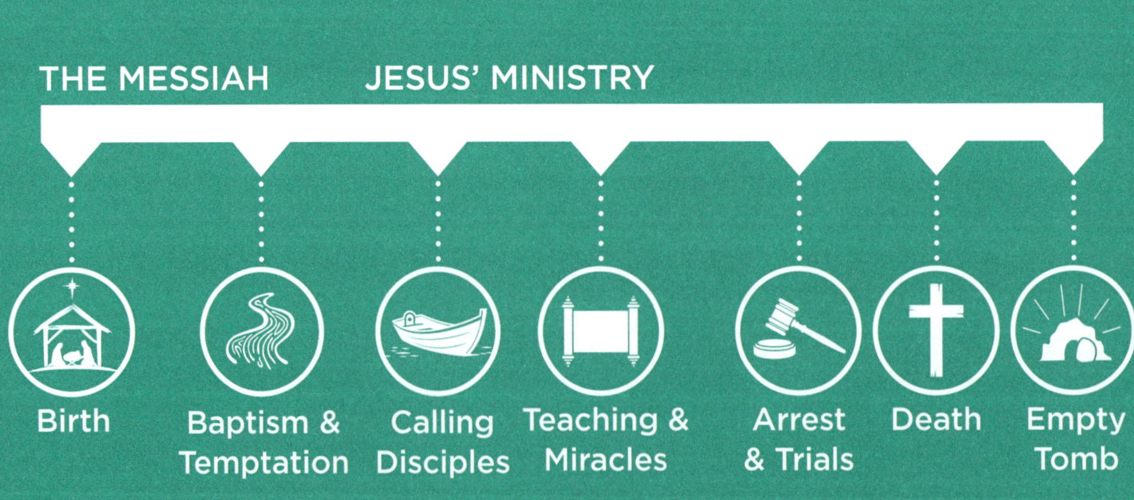

Discuss [35 MINUTES]

Discuss what you just watched by answering the following questions.

1. What was God doing during the "four hundred years of silence" to prepare the gospel to be spread to the known world? What does this say about what he is likewise doing during the times of silence in our lives?

2. Ask someone to read aloud Luke 4:14–21. What was Jesus announcing when he stood up in the synagogue in Nazareth and read the prophecy from Isaiah? What does this prophecy reveal about the nature of God's kingdom that Jesus had come to usher in on earth?

3. The phrase "good news" in the first century was an announcement or proclamation that a change in leadership had happened. Given this, what would this phrase have meant to the Jewish and Roman audience of Jesus' time? What would they have understood Jesus was doing when he announced the "good news" that God's kingdom had come to the earth?

4. Ask someone to read aloud Hebrews 10:1–4 and 11–14. Jesus died on the cross at the same time that thousands of people were gathering in the temple for the slaughter of the Passover lamb. Why is this significant? What did Jesus—the perfect Passover Lamb—accomplish through his death that could not be accomplished through the sacrifice of animals?

5. Ask someone to read 1 Corinthians 15:12–19. Everything changed when Jesus conquered death and hell. What does Paul say is the importance of the resurrection of Jesus when it comes to our faith? What hope do all those who put their faith in Jesus have because of what he accomplished by the resurrection?

Respond [10 MINUTES]

Jesus was 100 percent man and 100 percent God. This truth can be difficult for us to wrap our minds around. How could Jesus be *completely* human while also being *completely* divine? Furthermore, what bearing does this have on our faith? The author of Hebrews provides us with an important clue. Read the following passage and then answer the questions that follow.

> 14 Therefore, since we have a great high priest who has ascended into
> heaven, Jesus the Son of God, let us hold firmly to the faith we profess.
> 15 For we do not have a high priest who is unable to empathize with
> our weaknesses, but we have one who has been tempted in every
> way, just as we are—yet he did not sin. 16 Let us then approach God's
> throne of grace with confidence, so that we may receive mercy and
> find grace to help us in our time of need.
>
> **HEBREWS 4:14–16**

How does Jesus' humanity enable him to understand the temptations you face in this life?

Jesus is your "high priest" in that he intercedes for you before God (see Hebrews 7:25). What does the author of Hebrews say this allows you to do with confidence?

Pray [10 MINUTES]

When it is time to close this session, take a moment to pray with your group. Give thanks to God for sending his Son, Jesus, to be the final Passover Lamb and perfect sacrifice for your sins. Ask Jesus to help you overcome the temptations you face, knowing that he understands what you are facing. Ask God to continue to work in your heart to share the good news with others.

SESSION FIVE

PERSONAL STUDY

The time of waiting had finally ended. The promised Messiah had arrived. He was God-in-the-flesh who "made his dwelling among us" (John 1:14). He announced that "the kingdom of heaven has come near" (Matthew 4:17). Yet this kingdom was unlike anything the Israelites had expected. It would not be a political kingdom where the mighty rule and the elite are praised. In this personal study, you will dig deeper into the ministry of Jesus and explore how the Gospels portrayed his mission and legacy. As you work through the exercises, write down your responses to the questions, as you will be given a few minutes to share your insights at the start of the next session if you are doing this study with others. If you are reading *The Bible, Simplified* alongside this study, first review chapters 24–32 in the book.

ISRAEL IN JESUS' DAY

STUDY 1 | The Four Gospels

Think about a story from your past that is often retold by your friends or family. The story changes depending on who is telling it. Your uncle remembers it one way. Your mother a different way. One friend remembers certain details of what happened. Another friend recalls a completely different set of events. All of this is to be expected. When there are multiple witnesses, there are often multiple versions of the same tale.

The Gospels are a bit like this. If you don't know what the Gospels are before reading them, you might get a sense of déjà vu once you get to Mark and Luke. *Didn't I just read about feeding the five thousand? Didn't Jesus already raise that person from the dead?* This is because a large percentage of the stories found in the first three Gospels, known as the "Synoptic Gospels," overlap. While John contains more unique content, it also includes accounts of Jesus' death and resurrection and other significant stories found in the Synoptic accounts.

While all the Gospels share common stories of Jesus, they are written a bit (and, at times, a *lot*) differently. Different authors writing from different perspectives to different audiences and at different times will naturally result in different versions of the same story. However, these differences do not discredit the truth of what has been written. Think about your old family stories. Just because there are different perspectives on what happened doesn't mean the events didn't happen.

In fact, when it comes to the Gospels, many theologians think it's the differences in them that gives them credence. As one commentator notes, "If anything, it bolstered claims, showing that the accounts were not made up and rehearsed. When we think of multiple people conferring to align their stories perfectly, we tend to think of criminals before interrogation, not eyewitnesses to a world-altering event."[13] Matthew, Mark, Luke, and John weren't trying to coerce or manipulate their audiences with their narratives. They were simply relating accounts of what had happened based either on their own personal experiences with Jesus or on the experiences of those who had walked closely with Jesus during his time on earth.

When you read the Gospels, you can cross-reference them to fill in gaps in the story and gather more details about an event. They work together, illuminating different parts of Jesus' work. They each help to paint a fuller picture of who Jesus was then and who he is to us today.

SCRIPTURE: Matthew 28:1–8; Mark 16:1–8; Luke 24:1–12; John 20:1–14

OBSERVATION

1. After you have read each of these passages, fill out the table below to compare and contrast each version of the story of the empty tomb.

QUESTION	MATTHEW	MARK	LUKE	JOHN
Who first saw the empty tomb?				
What did they do after seeing the empty tomb?				
Who appeared to the women and what did they say?				
Is Peter mentioned? If so, what did he do?				

2. Lee Strobel remarked, "[The resurrection] is the basis of Christian hope. It's the miracle of all miracles."[14] Jesus' resurrection is *pivotal* to the Christian faith. Given this, why do you think each retelling of the empty tomb story is different? What do you think these differences do to the validity of Jesus' resurrection?

APPLICATION

3 How much do you know about the Gospels? Check the statement that best applies to you.

- ❑ I didn't even know what the Gospels were until this session.
- ❑ I've read them but haven't studied them.
- ❑ I've done a few Bible studies on the Gospels but wish I knew more.
- ❑ I've studied each Gospel thoroughly and understand their similarities and differences.

4 Why are the stories of Jesus' teachings, miracles, and other acts in the Gospels so important to the Christian faith? How have they impacted your own faith?

5 Which of the four Gospels are you interested in studying more? Write down a plan that would help you study that Gospel over the next thirty days.

My plan for studying this Gospel:

____

____

____

____

____

____

PRAYER

God, thank you for your Word, and thank you for the Gospels that tell the story of my Savior. Guide me as I study the Gospels. Point out the truths that you want me to absorb into my life. Please continue your work in changing my heart to be more like Jesus. Amen.

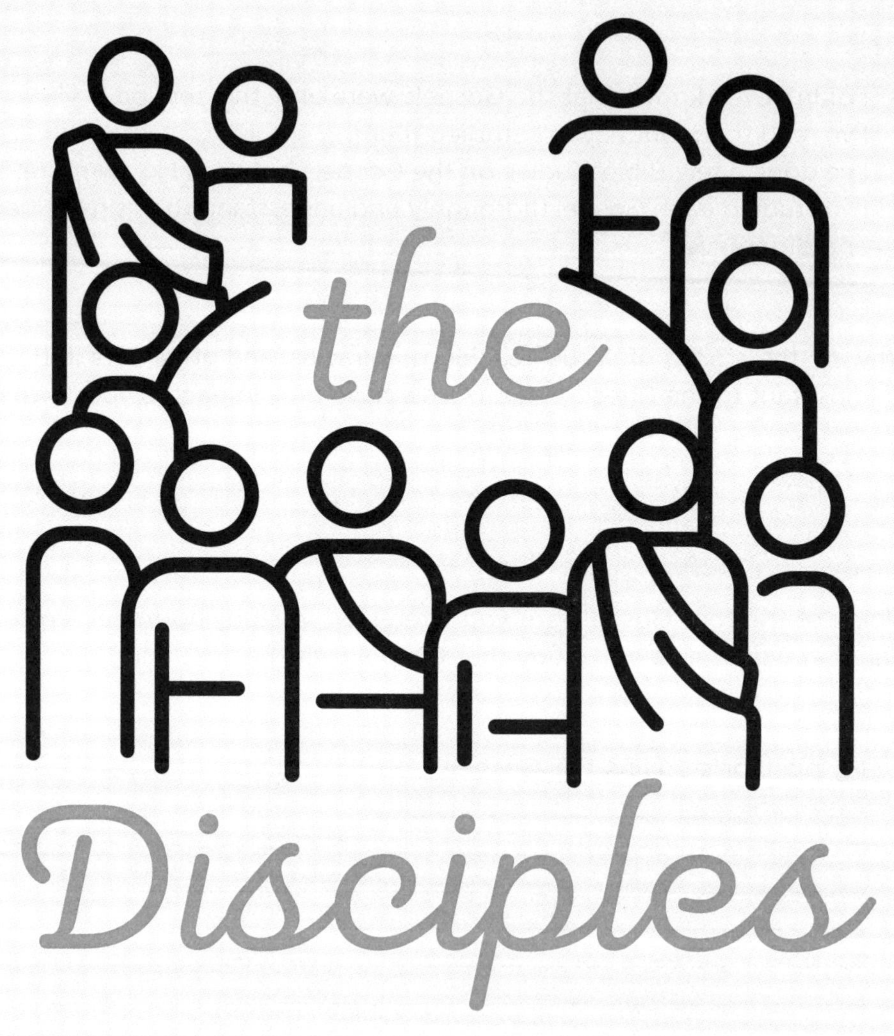
the
Disciples

STUDY 2 | True Disciples of Jesus

Who was your childhood hero—someone you admired, revered, and wanted to be like? How did you mimic your hero? Maybe you dressed like him. Maybe you tried to talk like her. Maybe you told everyone that you were going to be just like this person one day.

This is how disciples felt about their rabbis during Jesus' time. They did not simply respect them but wanted to be *like* them. They mimicked their rabbis through their speech and writing—teaching as their rabbi would and acting as he would. Jesus' disciples would have done the same. We tend to think of them as companions of Jesus, but actually they were students of his. They absorbed his every word, learned to interpret Scripture as he did, and perhaps even practiced how to teach it in the same way he would.

Of Jesus' twelve disciples, the ones we most often read about are Simon (Peter), Andrew, James, and John. All four were fishermen when Jesus asked them to follow him. In that day, fishing offered a good and steady paycheck, especially when compared to those working the land.[15] In addition, these men were likely carrying on the family business, so leaving that business would have been a sign of disrespect to their families.[16] Still, these men decided to follow Jesus as their rabbi, meaning they devoted their time, study, and lives to him.

This is a more radical idea of discipleship than we have today. Rarely do we consider the implications of what it means to be a "disciple" of Christ. We don't often seek to mimic him in the same way as we did our childhood heroes. Yet when you look at the historical context, this is what a disciple was: a person fully dedicated to the rabbi and studying God's Word.

Following in the "dust" of our Rabbi means caring about him and his interpretation of God's Word above all else. It could mean leaving behind the security of a job or even a family in order to follow him. It means meditating on God's Word day and night. It is an all-in approach to faith. In a culture that prizes security over risk, money over poverty, and self-gain over selflessness, being a disciple of Jesus can feel counter to everything we've been taught. Yet being a disciple of Jesus is what we have all been called to be.

SCRIPTURE: Mark 1:16–20

OBSERVATION

1 When leaders look for "disciples" today, they often offer lengthy explanations about their own qualities and why it would be a good idea for others to follow them. However, this is not the approach Jesus took in choosing his disciples.

How did Jesus seek his disciples?

What was the offer Jesus made to Simon and Andrew?

2 Going a little farther, Jesus saw two more fishermen preparing their nets.

What do we read about how Jesus called them?

How did all four of them respond to Jesus' invitation?

APPLICATION

3 How has Jesus "called" you to be his disciple? Was there a specific time and place that you remember receiving that call? Explain your response.

4 One of the things that set the twelve disciples apart from all the others who said that they *wanted* to be Christ's disciples is that they were willing to leave everything behind in the moment. What does this say about what Jesus desires in his disciples today?

5 What is one step you could take today to be a more devoted disciple of Jesus?

PRAYER

Dear God, give me the courage to follow Jesus. Some days it's easy. Other days it's difficult. But please help me follow after him no matter what—even when I'm afraid and even when I'm not sure of what's next. Make me a true disciple of your Son. Amen.

GOD'S KINGDOM

ON EARTH

STUDY 3 | A Spiritual Overthrow

In the Old Testament, God often showed up for his people by defeating their enemies. These were often powerful people groups like the Egyptians (see Exodus 14), the Canaanites (see Judges 1), and the Assyrians (see 2 Kings 19). God helped his people win wars—it was how he ensured the security of his people. So, naturally, when the Israelites learned that the Lord was sending a Messiah, they expected a great warrior like Joshua, or Gideon, or Samson, or David. They expected a powerful leader who would defeat their enemies in battle.

What they were *not* expecting was for the Messiah to be born in a small town, into a humble Jewish family (with no ties to nobility), and to lead an early life unnoticed by most. In fact, little is known about Jesus' life until he begins his public ministry at the age of thirty. In all the Gospels, there is just one story of Jesus when he was twelve (see Luke 2:41–52), which contains this footnote: "And Jesus grew in wisdom and stature, and in favor with God and man" (verse 52).

Jesus did not grow up being trained in conquest and war. In fact, what we find when Jesus does begin his ministry is quite the opposite. He tells the crowds, "You have heard that it was said, 'Eye for eye, and tooth for tooth.' But I tell you, do not resist an evil person. If anyone slaps you on the right cheek, turn to them the other cheek also" (Matthew 5:38–39). He proclaims that in God's kingdom, the meek inherit the earth, the merciful are shown mercy, the pure in heart see God, the peacemakers are called God's children, and the persecuted receive the kingdom of heaven (see 5:5–10).

Jesus' announcement of the kingdom he was bringing to earth was upside down to what God's people were anticipating. This is why it was difficult for those like the Pharisees, the religious elite, to believe that Jesus was the Messiah. He wasn't acting very king-like, at least according to their views. Jesus came to conquer people's hearts—not Rome. He came to free people from sin, not empirical oppressors (though Jesus spoke against those who oppressed). His battle was with the spiritual realm more than with an earthly regime. While governments come and go, his government would always remain and his kingdom would always reign.

The people misunderstood Jesus. We often do the same. This is why it is critical for us to ask what it really means to live like Jesus. What it means for him to be in our hearts. And what it means to live as his kingdom people here . . . now . . . today.

SCRIPTURE: Matthew 5:1–12, 17–19; Luke 6:20–23

OBSERVATION

1. This teaching from Jesus is from a sermon that he gave on a "mountainside" or "level place" likely overlooking the Sea of Galilee. After you have read Matthew 5:1–12 and Luke 6:20–23, fill out the table below to compare Jesus' teaching in these two accounts.

QUESTION	MATTHEW	LUKE
Who is blessed and what do they receive?	verse 3	verse 20
Who is blessed and what do they receive?	verse 6	verse 21
Who is blessed and what do they receive?	verse 4	verse 21
Who is blessed and what do they receive?	verses 11–12	verses 22–23

2. Fill in the blanks: "Do not think that I have come to ________ the Law or the Prophets; I have not come to ________ them but to ________ them" (Matthew 5:17).

How did Jesus accomplish this?

Who is considered the "least" and the "greatest" in his kingdom?

APPLICATION

3. When it comes to living under God's kingdom, as defined in the passages above, what is the most challenging aspect for you? What makes this so difficult?

4. What is the most hopeful aspect about God's kingdom for you? What would our world be like if people actually embraced the principles that Jesus is proclaiming?

5. When you look at the characteristics of those whom Jesus says will be blessed in his kingdom, which of them describe your life or your situation?

PRAYER

Father, thank you for sending your Son to conquer my heart. Thank you for the way that you have established your kingdom on earth. I ask today that you will give me wisdom as I live according to your kingdom's rules, not according to the world's. In Jesus' name, amen.

CONNECT AND DISCUSS

Connect with a fellow group member and discuss some of the key insights from this session. Use any of the following prompts to help guide your discussion.

1. What especially stood out to you about what God was doing to prepare the way for the gospel during the four hundred years of silence?

2. What most inspired you about Jesus' life? What most challenged you?

3. How have the previous weeks' studies about the Old Testament helped you understand the Gospels and the material covered during this week's study?

4. How have you embraced what it means to be a disciple of Jesus? How can you encourage each other to continue to grow as Jesus' disciples?

CATCH UP AND READ AHEAD

Use this time to go back and complete any of the study and reflection questions from previous days that you weren't able to finish. Make a note below of any revelations you've had and reflect on any growth or personal insights you've gained.

Read chapters 33–36 in *The Bible, Simplified* before the next group gathering. Use the space below to make note of anything in those chapters that stands out to you, inspires you, or encourages you.

Schedule | Week 6

BEFORE GROUP MEETING	Read chapters 33–36 in *The Bible, Simplified* Read the Welcome section (page 112)
GROUP MEETING	Discuss the Connect questions Watch the video teaching for session 6 Discuss the questions that follow as a group Do the closing exercise and pray (pages 112–116)
STUDY 1	Complete the personal study (pages 119–121)
STUDY 2	Complete the personal study (pages 123–125)
STUDY 3	Complete the personal study (pages 127–129)
CONNECT AND DISCUSS	Connect with one or two group members Discuss the follow-up questions (page 130)
CATCH UP AND READ AHEAD (before week 7 group meeting)	Read chapters 37–39 in *The Bible, Simplified* Complete any unfinished studies (page 131)

SESSION SIX

The Early Church

As followers of Jesus, it is our responsibility to continue spreading the message of God's kingdom in every way possible—past Jerusalem, Judea, Samaria, and into the rest of the world. We have the stories of the early church in Acts and the letters of Paul and others in the New Testament to serve as our inspiration, guide, and motivation.

Welcome [READ ON YOUR OWN]

It is easy for us to take the New Testament for granted. After all, we've always had it available to us to learn about Jesus' life, about the church, and about the way in which we are to live before God. Yet this was not the case for the first Christians—those known as followers of "the Way" (Acts 9:2). They had the Torah and other Hebrew texts of the Old Testament, which they likely read in Greek (a translation known as "the Septuagint"). But they didn't have the Gospels, or the book of Acts, or the epistles that we have in the New Testament.

These early followers of Jesus had only the instructions of the leaders that God had put in place to know how they should live. This is why the earliest parts of the New Testament are actually *letters* from leaders like Paul or James to these groups of believers. These letters were read aloud, copied, and then distributed to other congregations as the church began to spread from Jerusalem to Judea to Samaria and the rest of the world. Furthermore, just as God did with the Israelites, he did not leave these early believers to fend for themselves. He sent his Spirit to guide them, encourage them, and give them discernment when they needed it most.

In the Old Testament, the temple was the dwelling place of God (see 1 Kings 8:11). But now God's Spirit dwells in the lives of those who put their faith in Christ. We are "God's temple" (1 Corinthians 3:16). No tabernacle or temple required. No velvet curtain dividing us from the divine. Because of Jesus, the Holy Spirit lives within us. So, as you study about the Holy Spirit and how he worked in the disciples' lives to build the church, think about how he might be guiding you today to do the work of Christ in the local and global church.

Connect [10 MINUTES]

Get this session started by choosing one or both of the following questions to discuss together as a group:

- What is something that spoke to you in last week's personal study that you would like to share with the group?

— or —

- Who is the Holy Spirit to you? What role does the Spirit play in your life?

Watch [25 MINUTES]

Now watch the video for this session. Below is an outline of the key points covered during the teaching. Record any key concepts that stand out to you.

OUTLINE

I. What role did the Holy Spirit play in establishing the early church?

A. Before Jesus ascended into heaven, he told his disciples they would receive power from the Holy Spirit to be his witnesses on earth.

B. On Pentecost, as the disciples and others gathered together in an upper room in Jerusalem, the Holy Spirit came in the form of *wind* and *fire*.

C. In the Old Testament, the presence of God manifested in wind and fire. Now, God was saying his presence would indwell every believer in Jesus.

II. How did the church grow and spread throughout Judea and Samaria?

A. Peter, filled with the Holy Spirit, preached the first sermon.

B. Peter revealed to his Jewish audience that Jesus was the next step in their faith. On that day, three thousand people were added to the church.

C. Tensions in Jerusalem mounted, as many of the Jews (especially the religious leaders) believed the message of the early believers to be blasphemous.

D. Stephen became the church's first martyr. A persecution broke out, led by a man named Saul, that scattered the followers of Jesus.

III. What led to Saul becoming an apostle of Jesus?

A. Saul went to Damascus to arrest followers of Jesus who had fled there. On the way he encountered the risen Jesus, and his life was forever changed.

B. Saul, whose Roman name was Paul, ended up preaching the gospel in Damascus. He then joined forces with a leader named Barnabas in Antioch.

IV. How did Paul begin to spread the gospel to the world?

A. Paul, Barnabas, and other co-workers were commissioned to go on a series of "missionary journeys" to spread the gospel in Asia Minor and Greece.

B. Meanwhile, many Jewish believers were having troubling getting over the fact that God would allow Gentiles into his plan. This was ultimately resolved at a council in Jerusalem.

C. Paul wrote letters to the churches he established to explain how to live like Jesus and be in community with one another. These letters make up a large part of the New Testament.

D. Our commission is the same as these early followers—to spread the message of God's kingdom to every corner of the world.

NOTES

EARLY CHURCH
Ascension
Birth of Church
Persecution
Saul (Conversion)
Missionary Journeys

Discuss [35 MINUTES]

Discuss what you just watched by answering the following questions.

1. Ask someone to read aloud Acts 2:1–13. How many people groups heard Jesus' disciples speaking in their native tongues? Why was this significant?

2. In the Old Testament, God led the Israelites through a pillar of fire (see Exodus 13:21). The prophet Ezekiel also recorded a vision in which the "wind" of God's Spirit blew over a valley of dry bones and filled them with new life (see Ezekiel 37:9–14). How do these images help you understand what was happening to followers of Jesus on the Day of Pentecost?

3. Ask someone to read Acts 7:54–60. Stephen, a deacon in the early church, was the first to be martyred for his faith in Christ. What did Stephen witness when he looked up to heaven? How did his words further infuriate the Jewish religious leaders?

4. Ask someone to read aloud Acts 8:1–3 and 9:1–20. What stands out about Paul's conversion story? How did God use him—even while he was persecuting followers of Jesus—to complete his mission of spreading the gospel to Jerusalem, Judea, Samaria, and beyond?

5. Paul and his co-workers would visit a city, plant a church there, and then move on to the next location in need of the gospel. Paul would then receive reports of how the church was doing and respond to any questions they had. How does this explain the structure of the books of the New Testament called the "epistles"? Why do you think the churches who received Paul's letters copied and preserved them so that we have them today?

Respond [10 MINUTES]

In the past, the presence of God was contained to one location—the tabernacle/temple—where the heavenly realm overlapped the earthly realm. However, after the coming of the Holy Spirit at Pentecost, the temple would now be "inside" every follower of Jesus. For this reason, believers in Christ needed to carefully consider how they were living. Read the following statement from Paul on this and then answer the questions that follow.

> [17] Whoever is united with the Lord is one with him in spirit [18] Flee from
> sexual immorality. All other sins a person commits are outside the
> body, but whoever sins sexually, sins against their own body. [19] Do you
> not know that your bodies are temples of the Holy Spirit, who is in
> you, whom you have received from God? You are not your own; [20] you
> were bought at a price. Therefore honor God with your bodies.
>
> **1 CORINTHIANS 6:17–20**

How should knowing that your body is a temple of the Holy Spirit impact the choices you make each day?

What does Paul mean when he says that you were "bought at a price"? Why should this compel each of us to "therefore honor God with your bodies"?

Pray [10 MINUTES]

When it is time to close this session, take a moment to pray with your group. Ask the Holy Spirit to be present with you this week and give you the guidance, wisdom, and strength you need. Pray that the Lord would help you to view your body as the temple of the Holy Spirit. Finally, thank God for giving you access to him through the sacrifice of Jesus and the work of the Spirit.

SESSION SIX

PERSONAL STUDY

Among Jesus' final instructions to his disciples was this command: "Go and make disciples of all nations, baptizing them in the name of the Father and of the Son and of the Holy Spirit, and teaching them to obey everything I have commanded you" (Matthew 28:19–20). The faithful followers of Jesus soon got to work in fulfilling this great commission. Missionaries like Paul, Barnabas, Silas, Timothy, and Titus spread the gospel to Gentile lands. Paul and others wrote letters to the new believers, instructing them on how to live as members of God's family. Yet this process did not come without its challenges. As you work through the following exercises, write down your responses to the questions, as you will be given a few minutes to share your insights at the start of the next session if you are doing this study with others. If you are reading *The Bible, Simplified* alongside this study, first review chapters 33–36 in the book.

PAUL'S MISSIONARY JOURNEYS

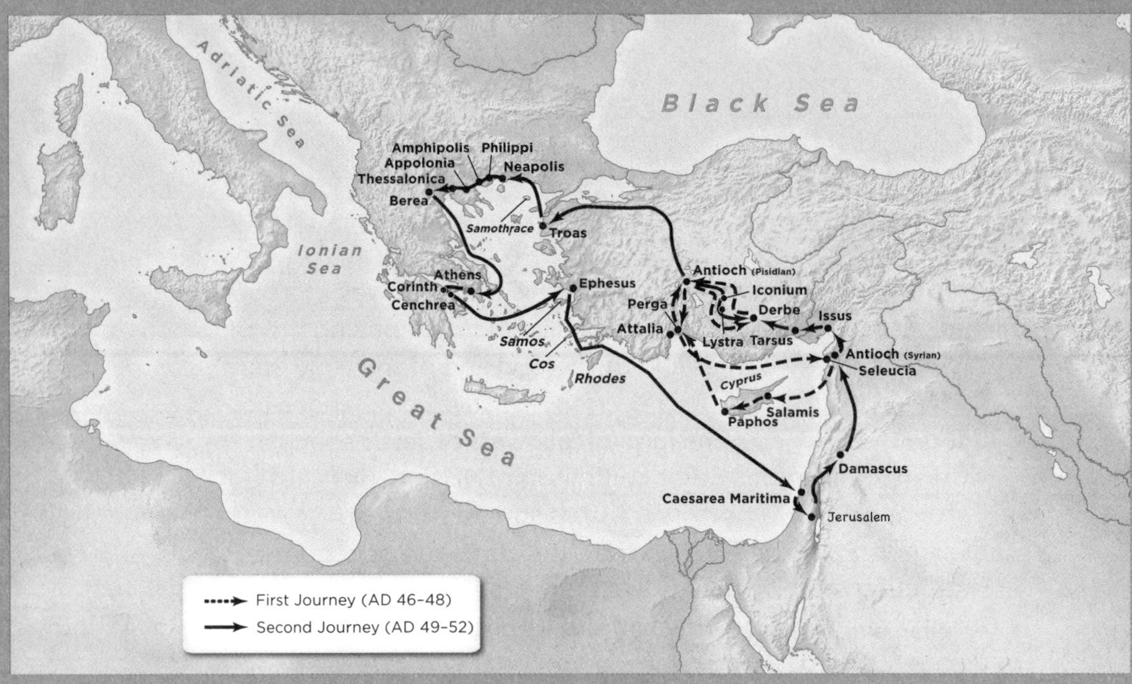

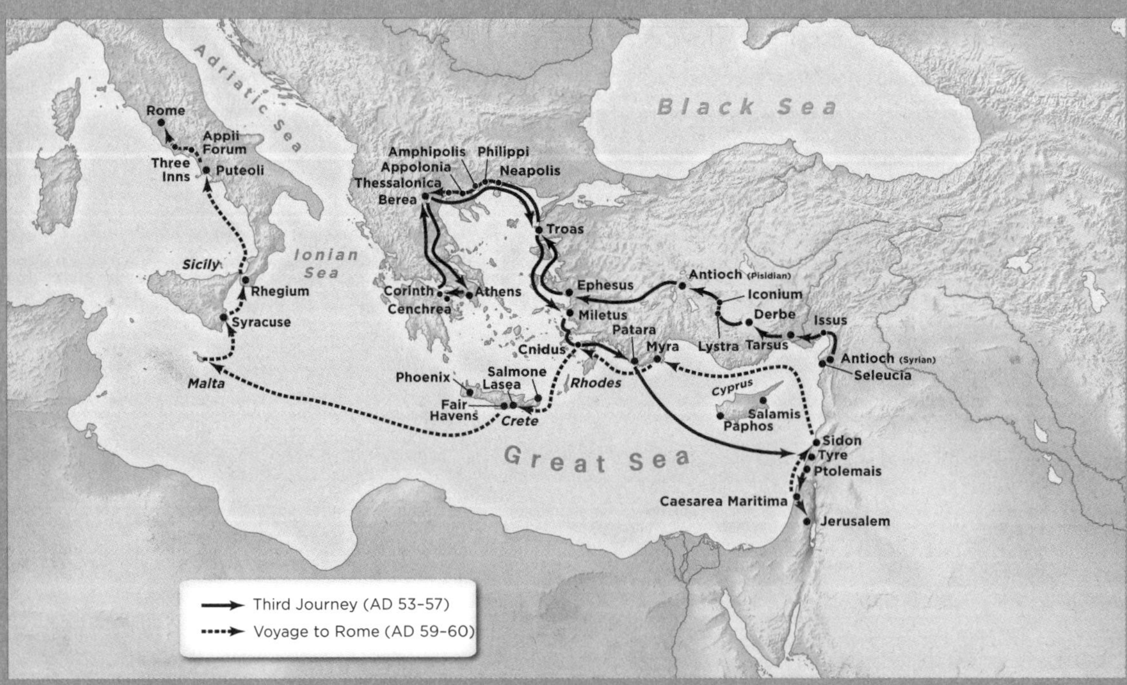

STUDY 1 | The First Missionaries

If you are part of a church that focuses on worldwide missions, you know of missionaries who have been to places all over the globe. These men and women have taken up Jesus' commission to preach the message of salvation to *everyone*, and they can be found *everywhere* from America to Europe to Africa to Asia . . . and beyond.

It is hard to say who was the *first* Christian missionary. Some say the Samaritan woman, who told her whole town about Jesus (see John 4:39). Some say Philip, a deacon in the early church, who was the first to be given the title "evangelist" (Acts 21:8). But certainly, we must consider Paul and Barnabas to be among those "first missionaries."

Paul and Barnabas's first mission is recorded in Acts 13–14. It spanned several cities along the coast of the Mediterranean. These cities would have been densely populated by diverse groups of people—an ideal setting for spreading God's Word.[17] The journey had its ups and downs. Paul and Barnabas converted many Jews, spread hope to the Gentiles, and "won a large number of disciples" (Acts 14:21). Yet they were also persecuted. In Lystra, the Jews stoned Paul and dragged him out of the city (see verse 19). In Iconium, Paul and Barnabas discovered a plot against them—one devised by both Jews and Gentiles—and were forced to flee the city.

The miracles the duo performed were met with mixed responses. Some of the people believed in Jesus as a result. But some believed in Barnabas and Paul and wanted to perform sacrifices for them. This caused the two missionaries to plead, "We too are only human, like you. We are bringing you good news, telling you to turn from these worthless things to the living God, who made the heavens and the earth and the sea and everything in them" (verse 15).

Through it all, Paul and Barnabas remained faithful to the message and brought many people to salvation. As the "first missionaries," they remain an inspiration to countless missionaries today, especially those who are called to places where the message of Christ could be met with hostility

Of course, you don't have to be called to global missions to be a missionary or to be inspired by Paul and Barnabas's work. All Christians are called to be disciples and to make disciples. You can be a missionary in your own home, school, and workplace—living out God's message and inviting others into the love and fellowship of Christ.

SCRIPTURE: Acts 13:38-52

OBSERVATION

1. This passage is the end of a sermon that Paul gave on the Sabbath in a place called Pisidian Antioch.

How did his audience initially respond to Paul's sermon?

What happened the next weekend when the Jews were present to hear Paul and Barnabas speak?

2. How did Paul and Barnabas respond to the criticism they received from these Jews? What does this say about whom God chooses to include in his kingdom?

APPLICATION

3. On a scale of 1 to 10, how likely are you to do **global** mission work—where you travel to a different country from your own and minister to the people there?

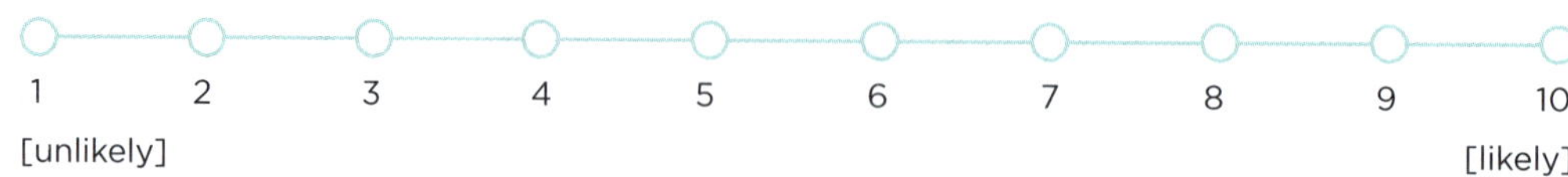

On a scale of 1 to 10, how likely are you to do **local** mission work—where you look for needs in your own country or community and minister to the people there?

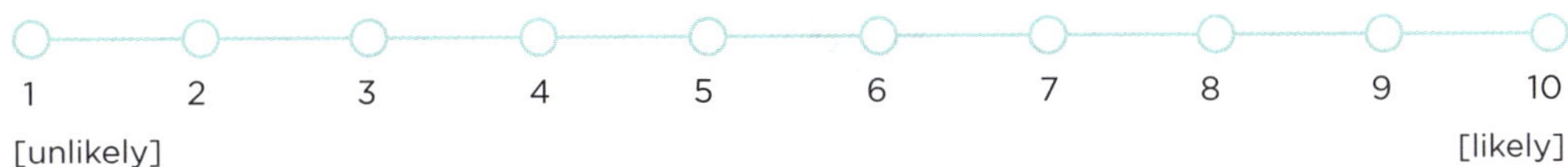

4 Why do you think Paul and Barnabas received such a mixed response from the Jews and Gentiles? What kind of responses have you received when sharing the gospel with others?

5 How does Paul and Barnabas's missionary journey encourage and challenge you? What more do you sense God is calling you to do when it comes to sharing about the message of Christ?

PRAYER

Father, I know your gospel is alive and well. Although the message of salvation has been spread far and wide, there are still unreached people groups and individuals all around me. Direct me in how I can spread the gospel to those people with the help of your Holy Spirit and the courage of all missionaries who have gone before me. In Jesus' name, amen.

WELCOME

STUDY 2 | Let in the Gentiles!

"We're sorry, but you just don't meet the qualifications to be part of our club." Have you ever received a letter (or email) like this? Even when it is something as trivial as wanting to join a social club, the rejection can feel hurtful. You wonder why you're not enough, or how you've fallen short or are in some way unworthy of the group's acceptance. And you may question the powers that be. *Who are they to say I'm not good enough to be in their club?*

We might question whether the early Gentile followers of Jesus felt the same way. They had also received a sort of "rejection letter" from the Jewish believers who did not feel it was appropriate for them to join the Christian faith—well, at least not until they converted to Judaism and began to follow the law. Why would these early Jesus followers be so selective? Why would they want to subject the Gentiles to such a strict code of conduct?

The reason is because of what these Jewish believers had learned in the Torah. God had told his people, "You are to be holy to me because I, the Lord, am holy, and I have set you apart from the nations to be my own" (Leviticus 20:26). The Jews considered the Gentiles to be unclean. So, the early followers of Jesus—who were Jewish—took the admittance of Gentiles seriously. The Gentiles threatened their holiness and, thus, their connection to God.

Fortunately, several of the early leaders in the church knew the Scriptures and prophecies that allowed the Gentiles to be part of God's plan. These were verses like Isaiah 49:6, in God which says to his prophet, "I will also make you a light for the Gentiles, that my salvation may reach to the ends of the earth." And Psalm 22:27–28: "All the ends of the earth will remember and turn to the Lord, and all the families of the nations will bow down before him, for dominion belongs to the Lord and he rules over the nations."

Allowing the Gentiles entrance into this newly forming religion was not a decision made by its early leaders. It was a fulfillment of the prophecy. Yet in spite of this biblical evidence, it took some convincing to officially allow the Gentiles to become followers of Jesus without first converting to Judaism. In fact, it took nothing less than a council in Jerusalem to decide once and for all if the hope that Jesus gave to the Jews was also to be extended to the Gentiles.

SCRIPTURE: Acts 15:1–21

OBSERVATION

1 The "certain people" who came to Antioch were Jewish believers who held that Gentiles must be "circumcised" (become Jews) in order to be saved. In the table below, write down what happened in each verse.

ACTION	PASSAGE
What claim did the Jewish believer make?	verse 1
How did Paul and Barnabas respond to this claim?	verse 2
How did the Antioch church address the matter?	verses 2–3
What happened when Paul and Barnabas met with the church in Jerusalem?	verse 4

2 What evidence did Peter provide that God had accepted the Gentiles into his family? How did he say both Jews and Gentiles are saved (see verses 7–11)?

3. James "the Just," who is believed to have been the half-brother of Jesus (see Galatians 1:9), was the leader of the Jerusalem church. How did he respond to Peter's claims? What did he say was to be in the "acceptance letter" that the church was to give to the Gentiles?

APPLICATION

4. What are some of the ways that we still exclude certain people groups from the church today? Why do you think the church has this tendency to decide who is "in" and who is out?

5. Even though we, as Christians, know we are saved by faith (see Ephesians 2:8), we can still be tempted to rely on the "law" or rules to make us feel secure in our salvation. Why do you think this desire to rely on rules is still so prevalent in the church today?

PRAYER

Dear God, thank you for including every tongue, tribe, and nation in salvation. Thank you that my salvation is secure through my faith in Jesus. Help me include others as I have been included. Help me live by grace when I try to live by the law. In your name I pray, amen.

STUDY 3 | A Final Letter

When you lose someone you love, having a record of that person's words in his or her own handwriting is invaluable. Letters your grandparents wrote each other. A card your mother sent to you while you were away at school. A postcard from your brother. There is something comforting about seeing a loved one's written words.

Timothy likely felt this way about Paul's final letter to him—which is widely believed among scholars to be the epistle of 2 Timothy. We know, at the least, that Paul wrote this letter from a Roman prison and that he knew the time for his departure was near (see 2:9; 4:6). In those last days of his life, he chose to write his final words to a friend.

In fact, Timothy was more like family to Paul. The apostle describes him as "my true son in the faith" (1 Timothy 1:2) and calls him "my dear son" (2 Timothy 1:2). Paul never married or had children (see 1 Corinthians 7:8), but we can assume Timothy was like a son to him. So Paul directed these final words to his son *in the faith*.

Remember, the Bible was written *for* us but not *to* us. In this letter, we are getting an intimate look into the relationship of a spiritual father and son—a mentor and his mentee. When someone writes to a beloved child for what might be the last time, that person is careful about what he or she says. In Paul's case, he was careful to choose words of instruction and words of encouragement for his son in the faith.

Paul reminded Timothy why they were doing the hard work they were doing of spreading the gospel: "Therefore I endure everything for the sake of the elect, that they too may obtain the salvation that is in Christ Jesus, with eternal glory" (2 Timothy 2:10). He encouraged Timothy to continue being a leader in the church and instructed him on how to "correct, rebuke and encourage" (4:2). And Paul reminded him of the value of Scripture: "From infancy you have known the Holy Scriptures, which are able to make you wise for salvation through faith in Christ Jesus. All Scripture is God-breathed and is useful for teaching, rebuking, correcting and training in righteousness, so that the servant of God may be thoroughly equipped for every good work" (3:15-17).

If these were the instructions that Paul chose to include in his final letter, we can assume they are important for us on how to lead the church, revere Scripture, and endure persecution when necessary. Paul did not write this letter *to* us . . . but it is certainly written *for* us.

SCRIPTURE: 2 Timothy 4:1–8

OBSERVATION

1 Write down the following actions that Paul gives to Timothy in verses 2 and 5:

_________ the word; be _____________ in season and out of season; ____________ ___________ and ___________________—with great ____________ and careful ______________. . . . But you, _________ your head in all situations, __________ hardship, _____ the work of an evangelist, _________ all the duties of your ministry.

2 What metaphors does Paul use in 2 Timothy 4:6–7 to describe his time spreading the gospel? Why do you think he described his actions in this way?

3 What did Paul know was in store for him after his time on this earth had come to an end? How do you think that Paul was able to maintain his focus on Christ in spite of his trials?

APPLICATION

4 What do you need to do in your life now so that you can confidently say, alongside Paul, that you "fought the good fight," "finished the race," and "kept the faith"?

"I fought the good fight . . ."

"I finished the race . . ."

"I kept the faith . . ."

5 If you knew your time on this earth was short, to whom would you write your final letter? What would you say? How would you encourage that person in the faith?

PRAYER

Heavenly Father, thank you for giving us your Word, which is good and useful for teaching. Help me to fight the good fight today. Give me courage, energy, and discernment as I live out the gospel, encourage others, and function as a leader to those around me. In Jesus' name, amen.

CONNECT AND DISCUSS

Connect with a fellow group member and discuss some of the key insights from this session. Use any of the following prompts to help guide your discussion.

1
What stood out to you about the differences in the disciples after the coming of the Holy Spirit on the Day of Pentecost?

2
The first recorded Christian sermon was given by Peter in Acts 2. What sermons have had a profound impact on you? Why?

3
Which of the epistles (Paul's or the general epistles) is your favorite? Why? Or which one would you like to study more—and why?

4
What common themes do you find are occurring in the Old and New Testaments? How do these themes apply to your faith today?

CATCH UP AND READ AHEAD

Use this time to go back and complete any of the study and reflection questions from previous days that you weren't able to finish. Make a note below of any revelations you've had and reflect on any growth or personal insights you've gained.

Read chapters 37–39 in *The Bible, Simplified* before the next group gathering. Use the space below to make note of anything in those chapters that stands out to you, inspires you, or encourages you.

Schedule | Week 7

BEFORE GROUP MEETING	Read chapters 37–39 in *The Bible, Simplified* Read the Welcome section (page 134)
GROUP MEETING	Discuss the Connect questions Watch the video teaching for session 7 Discuss the questions that follow as a group Do the closing exercise and pray (pages 134–138)
STUDY 1	Complete the personal study (pages 141–143)
STUDY 2	Complete the personal study (pages 145–147)
STUDY 3	Complete the personal study (pages 149–151)
CONNECT AND DISCUSS	Connect with one or two group members Discuss the follow-up questions (page 152)
CATCH UP AND READ AHEAD (before week 8 group meeting)	Read chapter 40 in *The Bible, Simplified* Complete any unfinished studies (page 153)

SESSION SEVEN

The End Times

Right now, in our world, everything is being impacted by sin. But one day, at the end of the age, everything will be restored to God's original intention. As followers of Christ, we can place our hope in this future when all of Creation—including us—will be restored and made new.

Welcome [READ ON YOUR OWN]

We all know that stories in books have a beginning, a middle, and an end. The end represents the resolution when the central conflict is resolved and all the loose ends are tied up. The book that we know as the Bible is, in many way, God's story of his interactions with us. It has a beginning (the garden of Eden) and a middle (the coming of Jesus). But the end of the Bible's story? It actually hasn't happened yet—and won't until Jesus returns to our world.

The Bible is clear that Christ *will* return. There *will* be an end to the story. The central conflict of our lives *will* be resolved when Satan is eternally removed from our reality. We just don't know *when* these end times will occur. As Jesus said to his followers, "The Son of Man will come at an hour when you do not expect him" (Matthew 24:44).

Perhaps you were raised in a church that centered on the end times and prophecies in the Bible like in Revelation. Or maybe you grew up in a tradition that hardly talked about the end times at all. The topic among Christians can be confusing, difficult, and even contentious to discuss. So why bother thinking about the end times at all? The reason is because the end of God's story is an important part of the overall story.

How you think about the *end* of days affects how you live *today*. If you think the whole heaven and hell thing is simply a concept in Scripture but not reality, you won't live as if you will face the final judgment. On the other hand, if you think the whole point of faith is to wait and look forward to heaven, you will miss God's kingdom on earth now. Jesus prayed, "Your kingdom come, your will be done, on earth as it is in heaven" (Matthew 6:10). Heaven *is* coming . . . but we are called to get to work in the meantime.

Connect [10 MINUTES]

Get this session started by choosing one or both of the following questions to discuss together as a group:

- What is something that spoke to you in last week's personal study that you would like to share with the group?

— *or* —

- When you think about heaven, what do you imagine? Where did this image or belief come from?

Watch [25 MINUTES]

Now watch the video for this session. Below is an outline of the key points covered during the teaching. Record any key concepts that stand out to you.

OUTLINE

I. **What is the apocalyptic literature in the Bible?**
   A. The Greek word means to uncover or reveal. Apocalyptic literature is a way that prophets reveal important truths about the spiritual realm to us.
   B. Daniel, Ezekiel, and Revelation are considered apocalyptic literature. They are meant to show us that God triumphs over sin in the end.
   C. We aren't meant to interpret the Bible based on the news. Rather, we read the Bible *first* and then see how it applies to what is going on around us.

II. **How should we read the book of Revelation?**
   A. We can't turn the book of Revelation into a timetable. It was written to give *hope* to those who were suffering persecution for their faith.
   B. Revelation has more than four hundred allusions to the Old Testament. Understanding those passages is critical for understanding Revelation.
   C. Jesus ends by saying, "I am coming soon" (Revelation 22:20). As modern readers, we hold on to that hope—just as the original recipients did.

III. **How should we understand heaven and hell?**
   A. Jesus is coming back to wipe out evil and finish the restoration of the world by incorporating the new heavens and new earth.
   B. This includes redeemed physical bodies for each of us. Believers will be judged for our good works. Unbelievers will be judged for their sin.
   C. Hell is eternal separation from God, but because of Jesus, anyone who has accepted his offer of *salvation* can be united with God for eternity.
   D. God gives a choice: heaven or hell. Putting our faith in Jesus is about participating in God's kingdom *now* in preparation of Jesus' future reign.

IV. **How should we understand the new heaven and new earth?**
   A. We aren't leaving this world behind to one day go to our "true" home in heaven far away.
   B. Eden was where God's dimension—heaven—collided with our dimension—earth. After the Fall, the heavenly realm split from the earthly realm.
   C. Jesus began the work of reuniting heaven and earth. When we live as people of God's kingdom, we are taking steps toward the same union.
   D. Heaven is the new Jerusalem—a full restoration of Eden. It is a place without sin, death, or pain . . . where we will live in perfect union with God again.

NOTES

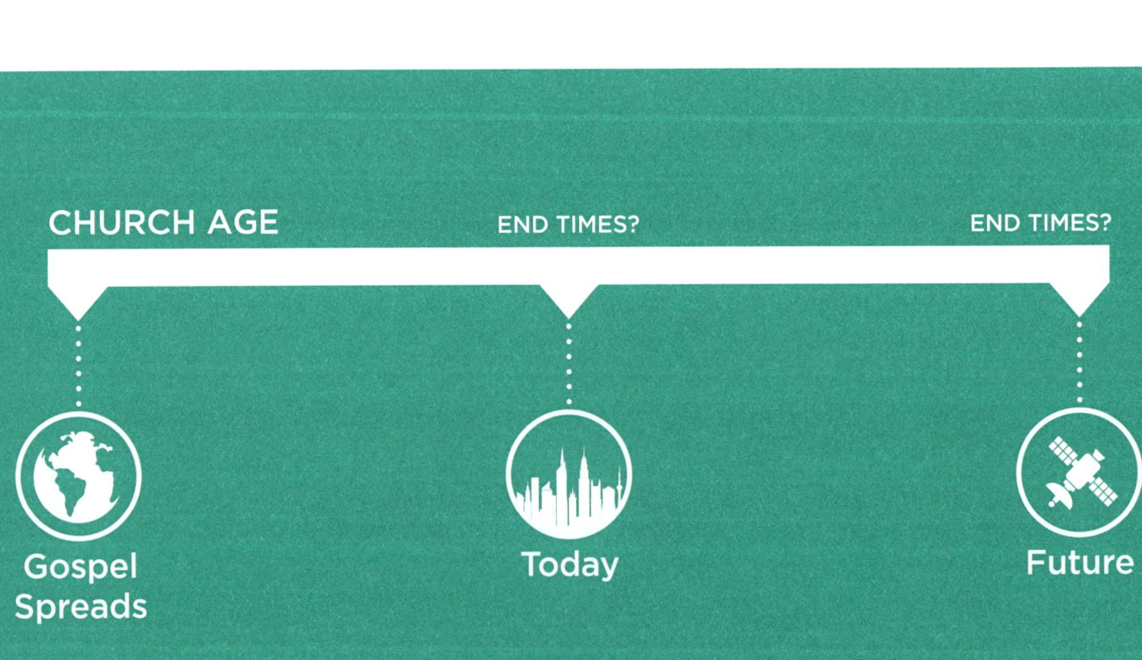

Discuss [35 MINUTES]

Discuss what you just watched by answering the following questions.

1 We are not meant to interpret the Bible based on what we see in the news. Rather, we are to read the Bible and see how it applies to our world. What is the danger in getting these two things mixed up? What problems could that create for us?

2 Ask someone to read aloud Revelation 1:9–11. It is important to understand that the book of Revelation was written by a real person (John) to real people (the believers in seven cities). How does John describe himself and his situation? What does this say about what he was facing as a faithful believer in Christ and what his readers were also facing?

3 Ask someone to read aloud Matthew 5:22, 8:11–12, and 13:41–42. No one likes to think about the reality of a hell. However, Jesus spoke of hell, so we—as his followers—should consider it as well. How did Jesus describe hell in these passages? Who is in danger of ending up there?

4 When Jesus arrives, it will be a time of judgment for both believers and non-believers. What feelings rise up in you when think of this judgment? How should the fact there will be a time of judgment impact how you choose to live your life?

5 Ask someone to read aloud Revelation 22:1–3. How do you see the restoration of God's original plan for this earth—what he established all the way back in the garden of Eden—in these verses? What "tree" is now available to all? What has been forever removed from our story?

Respond [10 MINUTES]

If hell is eternal separation from God, then heaven is eternal union with him. It's hard for us to imagine what that will be like—to live in perfect union with God in the new heaven and the new earth. However, we are given a glimpse of what this new existence will be like in John's vision. Read the follow description below and then answer the questions that follow.

> [1] Then I saw "a new heaven and a new earth," for the first heaven
> and the first earth had passed away, and there was no longer any
> sea. [2] I saw the Holy City, the new Jerusalem, coming down out of
> heaven from God, prepared as a bride beautifully dressed for her
> husband. [3] And I heard a loud voice from the throne saying, "Look!
> God's dwelling place is now among the people, and he will dwell
> with them. They will be his people, and God himself will be with
> them and be their God. [4] 'He will wipe every tear from their eyes.
> There will be no more death' or mourning or crying or pain, for the
> old order of things has passed away."
>
> **REVELATION 21:1–4**

In the new heaven and earth, there will no longer be a sea—no chaos. What is the significance of John describing the new Jerusalem as "a bride beautifully dressed for her husband"?

God's dwelling place will now be forever among his people. What promise from this passage do you need most today? What aspects give you the most hope today?

Pray [10 MINUTES]

When it is time to close this session, take a moment to pray with your group. Thank God for bringing his kingdom to earth. Thank Jesus that he is coming back. Pray that God will bring people into your life who are in desperate need of hearing the life-giving message of the gospel.

SESSION SEVEN
PERSONAL STUDY

You may have seen the title of this week's session and felt hesitant to dig in. The *end times*? The topic can be confusing, scary, even weird. But hopefully by now you feel a little more confident and curious about the topic. The Bible, after all, gives a lot of attention to end times, heaven, and hell. So, in this personal study, you explore more about what God's Word has to say about the end of the age and how these lessons apply to your life. Continue to write down your responses to the questions, as you will be given a few minutes to share your insights at the start of the next session if you are doing this study with others. If you are reading *The Bible, Simplified* alongside this study, first review chapters 37–39 in the book.

SEVEN CHURCHES OF REVELATION

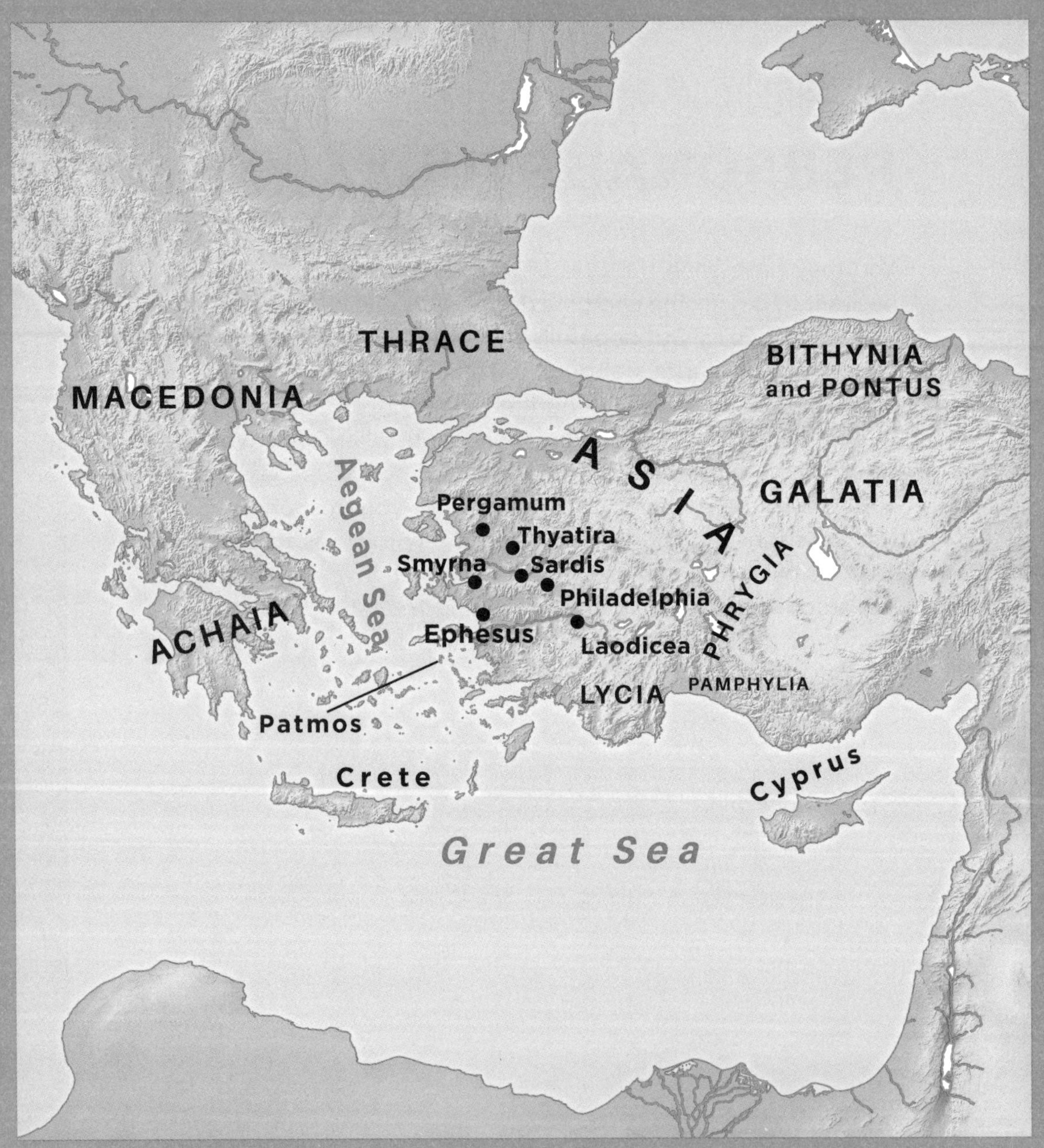

STUDY 1 | The Mark of Christ

To be a Christian is to believe there is more to this life than our physical realm. There is also a spiritual realm, and within it are powers of good and evil. With the power of the Holy Spirit, we can discern what is good and what is evil, but sometimes evil masquerades as good, and we get caught up doing the wrong thing.

This is one of the warnings John gives us in Revelation. In one part of his prophecy, he writes about two beasts: (1) the beast of the sea (see 13:1–10), and (2) the beast of the earth (see 13:11–18). The beast of the earth is as wicked as the beast of the sea, but it disguises itself with "horns like a lamb" while speaking "like a dragon" (verse 11). This beast is powerful. It wins over the people and deceives them. All of this sounds strange to us, but a little context can help us understand what this is all about.

The book of Revelation was written to an oppressed people group: the persecuted church under Roman rule. Religion in the Roman Empire was largely polytheistic, and the emperor was generally considered to be a god.[18] While Rome tolerated established religions like Judaism, newer religions like Christianity (which was suspiciously monotheistic) were less tolerated. As one scholar explains, "In the provinces, a number of cities were associated with certain deities. To reject these deities was in effect to reject the traditional power structures."[19]

Early Christians who preached the kingdom of Jesus, where "the last will be first, and the first will be last" (Matthew 20:16), threatened the traditional power structures and, therefore, the empire. They did not worship Caesar; they worshiped God.

The final description John gives of the beast of the earth is that he will put his mark on people so everyone knows who belonged to him. This mark was the number 666 (see Revelation 13:18). For John's Jewish audience, this would have had great significance. In Hebrew, every letter is associated with a number. The letters for Caesar Nero—one of the Caesars who caused great suffering for Christians—added up to 666.[20] It was a message to the Christians of John's day: Do not associate yourself with Caesar. Wear the mark of *Christ*, not the *beast*.

This is a valuable message for us as well. Whether we are living in the end times now or are far from them, beasts of the earth are alive and well. The temptation to follow after them, rather than after wisdom, remains a danger to Christians all over the world.

SCRIPTURE: Revelation 2:12–17; Numbers 25:1–5

OBSERVATION

1. The book of Revelation is addressed to a specific audience—seven churches in the Roman province of Asia (see Revelation 1:4). In Revelation 2–3, Jesus instructs John to write messages to each of these churches. One of the letters is to a church located in the city of Pergamum. What does Jesus say about the place where the believers in Pergamum live? How does he describe the city (see 2:13)?

2. The phrase "where Satan has his throne" (verse 13) refers to the fact that Pergamum was a center of pagan worship—especially the worship of the Roman emperors. (A temple dedicated to the worship of Emperor Augustus was constructed c. 29 BC.)[21] How does this shed light on the persecution these believers were facing? What tragedy had they witnessed?

3. Jesus nevertheless condemns some of the believers for holding "to the teaching of Balaam" (verse 14). Balaam's plan for defeating the Israelites is given in Numbers 25:1–5. How does this shed light on what these believers were doing?

APPLICATION

4 In Revelation 13:18, John writes, "Let the person who has insight calculate the number of the beast, for it is the number of a man. That number is 666." How does understanding the historical context help you understand the mark of the beast? How does it help you understand Jesus' message to the church in Pergamum?

5 Paul wrote that "Satan himself masquerades as an angel of light" (2 Corinthians 11:14). Write down five ways you've observed how Satan deceives people today.

1.
2.
3.
4.
5.

PRAYER

Father, may your Spirit guide me as I discern good from evil. Continue to give me wisdom and hope as I learn more about your Word. Help me to faithfully live the life you have called me to while I patiently wait for Jesus' return. In his name, I pray. Amen.

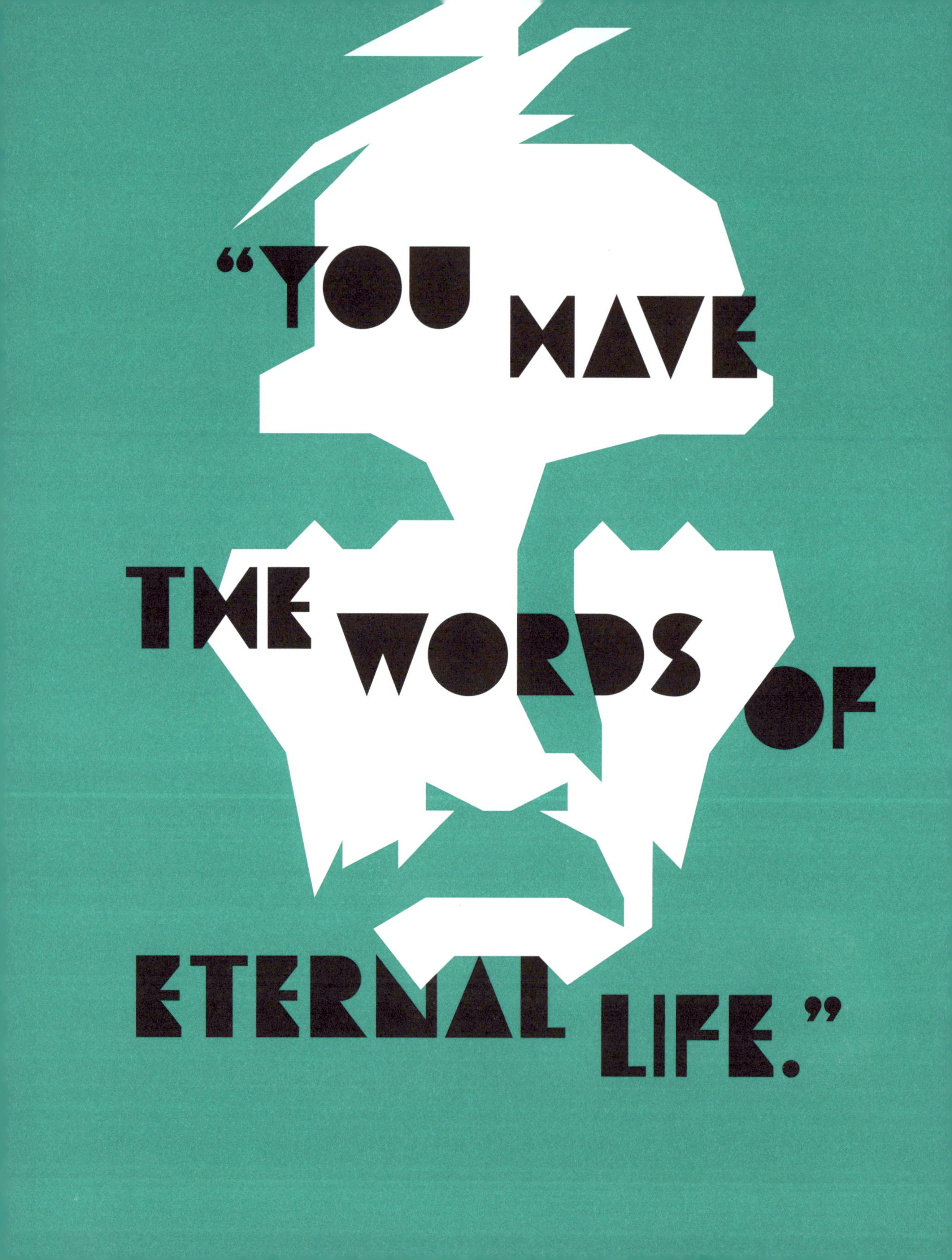

"You have the words of eternal life."

STUDY 2 | Your Kingdom Come

Imagine you were hired by a movie production company to help publicize a film. You love the film. It's beautiful, compelling, and heartbreaking. It tells the story of good triumphing over evil. You want everyone to know about this movie and to see it. So, on your first day of work, you show up to your office, sit at your desk, and do . . . nothing.

Around midday, your boss walks by and asks what you're doing. "Oh, nothing," you say. "Just waiting for the movie to release." Your boss might have some words about that.

God would too. When you became a Christian, you surrendered your life to Jesus, were fully forgiven for your sins, and received a promise of spending eternity with your heavenly Father. This is incredible news! But that's not the extent of the Christian life. You are not called to simply sit around and *wait* for heaven. Remember, heaven is not some far-off place. Heaven will be here, on earth, and it is your job *today* to help bring it here.

If you were hired to promote a movie that you loved and believed everyone should see . . . you would do just that. You would *promote* it. You would actually tell everyone you knew about it. You would compel them to go see it for themselves. You might even go around town and put up posters about the film. This is the same mindset that you need to adopt when it comes to sharing your faith.

In John's Gospel, we read of a time when many of Jesus' followers "turned back and no longer followed him" (6:66). Jesus turned to the twelve disciples and said, "You do not want to leave too, do you?" (verse 67). Peter answered, "Lord, to whom shall we go? You have the words of eternal life" (verse 68). If this is our attitude as well, then it should shape how we share those words with others.

Yes, we do this through evangelism—by sharing about what Jesus has done in our lives. But we also do it through our good works. We serve, encourage, donate, and get involved in causes that demonstrate our love for other people. Why? Because this type of work reflects the image of God. It brings heaven to earth.

We have all experienced heaven-meets-earth moments. Times when the love of God is palpable in us. Times of physical and spiritual healing. Times of reconciliation. Heaven on earth. There is no greater advertisement for Jesus than this. This is why we are called to accept Jesus as our Savior, then roll up our sleeves and get to work.

SCRIPTURE: Colossians 3:23–24; Ephesians 2:8–10; Titus 3:14; James 2:14–17

OBSERVATION

1 We promote Jesus not only through our evangelism but also through our good works. After you have read Colossians 3:23–24, Ephesians 2:8–10, and Titus 3:14, summarize what Paul says about the importance for believers in Christ to actively do good works.

PASSAGE	Why should followers of Jesus do good works?
Colossians 3:23–24	
Ephesians 2:8–10	
Titus 3:14	

2 According to James 2:14–17, what is the connection between faith and deeds? Why are words not enough when it comes to actively showing God's love to a person in need?

OBSERVATION

3 Paul states that we are saved "by grace . . . through faith" (Ephesians 2:8). However, we are also called "to do good works" (verse 10). How do you reconcile these two truths?

4 Who is someone you know who has lived out this area of their faith well—doing good works for God kingdom? What most inspires you about this person?

5 James goes so far as to say that "faith by itself, if it is not accompanied by action, is dead" (2:17). How does this inspire you to actively do good works and keep your faith "alive"?

PRAYER

Dear God, I know it is by grace that I have been saved. I also know that I am your handiwork, created to do good deeds. Show me what I can do today to help bring heaven to earth. May I never grow weary of doing good in your name. Amen.

OUR CHOICE

STUDY 3 | The Reality of Hell

What do you think about when you think of *hell*? Perhaps you would rather not think about it at all. Many would not. Hell is an unsavory topic. *Heaven* is so much nicer.

Jesus certainly spoke of heaven to his disciples. One time, he said to them, "My Father's house has many rooms; if that were not so, would I have told you that I am going there to prepare a place for you?" (John 14:2). We can picture the smile on their faces as they imagined the room they would have in God's heavenly mansion. These were pleasant and free-flowing conversations. Heaven is easy to talk about with others.

Yet Jesus didn't shy away from also talking about hell. In fact, he talked about it quite often. This is because Jesus cared about people not ending up there. On one occasion, he even made this startling statement: "If your hand causes you to stumble, cut it off. It is better for you to enter life maimed than with two hands to go into hell" (Mark 9:43). We can imagine this picture did *not* bring a smile to their faces.

The truth is that it is easier to talk about caring for the poor than it is to talk about the reality of hell. It is easier to talk about inviting others to church than it is to talk about hell. It is easier to talk about making sacrifices than it is to talk about hell. It is easier to talk about most anything other than hell. Perhaps this is why when it comes to hell, we tend to brush past those passages in our Bibles.

But whenever we feel this tension, it is an invitation to investigate the text rather than avoid it. We have come across something that doesn't make sense to us and we don't understand—and, as a result, it has made us afraid. The way we overcome this fear is through knowledge and understanding. As Paul wrote, "The Spirit God gave us does not make us timid, but gives us power, love and self-discipline" (2 Timothy 1:7).

God isn't afraid of our questions. In fact, it's our questions that allow us to get to know him better and understand his plan for our lives. So, what if you asked God about hell? What if you read the passages about it in the Bible? What if you got curious rather than afraid? The passages about hell could lead you to passages about heaven. The truth of eternal damnation could lead you to the truth of choice. Our God is no puppeteer. He has given us free will. So, no matter what your belief is about hell, or your past baggage around it, use this study as an invitation to lean in rather than run away. Trust that God will meet you in your questions.

SCRIPTURE: Matthew 10:26–33; Revelation 21:5–8

OBSERVATION

1 Jesus gave the instructions in Matthew 10:16–33 to his twelve disciples shortly after saying that he was sending them out "like sheep among wolves" (verse 16) and that they would "be flogged in the synagogues" (verse 17).

Why was there no need for the disciples to be afraid of these things?

What did Jesus say they were to fear instead (see verse 28)?

2 How did Jesus conclude this conversation with his disciples in verses 32–33? How would this have compelled them to be bold in sharing the message of Christ?

3 In Revelation 21:5–8, Jesus reveals what those "who are victorious" will one day inherit—"all of this." It's an amazing promise! But what does Jesus then reveal will happen to those who do *not* choose his path to victory?

APPLICATION

4 On a scale of 1 to 10, how comfortable do you feel discussing **heaven**?

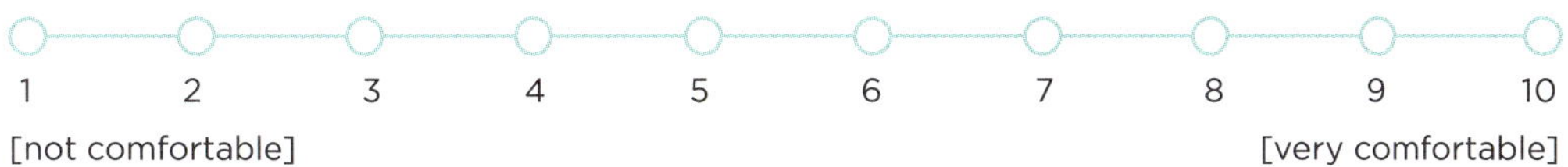

On a scale of 1 to 10, how comfortable do you feel discussing **hell**?

5 What do you find hopeful in the passages of Scripture that you've read this week? What do you find difficult, disturbing, or challenging? What questions do you have for God about your eternity? Take a moment to write them below.

PRAYER

Father in heaven, thank you for listening to my questions about the future. I confess that I am sometimes afraid and confused when I think about hell and heaven and what comes next. Give me your perfect peace and assurance today. Point me to passages from your Word that will help me better understand you and eternity. In Jesus' name, I pray. Amen.

CONNECT AND DISCUSS

Connect with a fellow group member and discuss some of the key insights from this session. Use any of the following prompts to help guide your discussion.

1. What is something new you learned about the end times in this session?

2. What is something you still find confusing about the end times?

3. What lessons from session 1, "Creation and Covenants," apply to this week's study about end times? What common themes do you see?

4. After thinking through your beliefs about the end times, heaven, and hell, how do you see those beliefs affecting your life and faith today?

CATCH UP AND READ AHEAD

Use this time to go back and complete any of the study and reflection questions from previous days that you weren't able to finish. Make a note below of any revelations you've had and reflect on any growth or personal insights you've gained.

Read chapter 40 in *The Bible, Simplified* before the next group gathering. Use the space below to make note of anything in those chapters that stands out to you, inspires you, or encourages you.

Schedule | Week 8

BEFORE GROUP MEETING	Read chapter 40 in *The Bible, Simplified* Read the Welcome section (page 156)
GROUP MEETING	Discuss the Connect questions Watch the video teaching for session 8 Discuss the questions that follow as a group Do the closing exercise and pray (pages 156–160)
STUDY 1	Complete the personal study (pages 163–165)
STUDY 2	Complete the personal study (pages 167–169)
STUDY 3	Complete the personal study (pages 171–173)
WRAP IT UP	Complete any unfinished personal studies (page 174) Connect with your group about the next study that you want to go through together

SESSION EIGHT

How to Be a Christian

As followers of Jesus, we should be walking so closely behind him that we get his "dust" on us every day—imitating him in how we think, pray, talk, act, and love. The closer we get to mimicking Jesus, the greater impact we will have for God's kingdom.

Welcome [READ ON YOUR OWN]

Over the course of this study, you've learned about each book of the Bible from Genesis to Revelation. You've followed the thread of God's story from Creation to the Fall to redemption through Jesus. You've uncovered common themes of covenant love and building God's kingdom. You've probably encountered stories that intrigued you, confused you, saddened you, and filled you with hope. You've read poetry, prose, prophecy, genealogies, and parables. Hopefully, the Bible feels more comprehensible now than it did before . . . and more mysterious.

Studying the Bible—especially studying it as a whole rather than just diving into individual books and select passages—opens up an entire world of God's love, provision, and purpose for your life. But your faith does not end with Bible study. In fact, studying is just the *beginning*. Just imagine going to medical school, studying your textbooks, taking every test, and then never practicing medicine on a patient. Never helping save a life or cure an illness. It's the same with Scripture. Applying what you've learned is how you put your faith into action, show others the love of God, and then invite them into the kingdom.

How do you do this? How do you take what is in this ancient book and put it into practice? You start small. You create daily habits that deepen your relationship with God and open your eyes to those around you. You pray, worship, and serve. And you don't just do this on Sundays. As a true follower of Jesus, you practice your faith each day, putting in at least a few minutes to be with him, learn from him, and follow him. He is your rabbi, and you are his disciple. He has so much more to show you. The Bible is just the beginning!

Connect [10 MINUTES]

Get this session started by choosing one or both of the following questions to discuss together as a group:

- What is something that spoke to you in last week's personal study that you would like to share with the group?

— *or* —

- What has stood out to you the most from this study of the Bible that you didn't know before? What impact has that had on you?

Watch [25 MINUTES]

Now watch the video for this session. Below is an outline of the key points covered during the teaching. Record any key concepts that stand out to you.

OUTLINE

I. **What are the next steps when it comes to your faith in Christ?**
   A. Discipleship is imitating Jesus in how you think, pray, talk, act, love, and grow closer to God.
   B. You have to be intentional in studying the Bible and seeking God in prayer.
   C. Transformation happens when you engage each day in "holy habits."

II. **What holy habits should you be incorporating into your life?**
   A. Prayer: One of the most common frameworks is called the ACTS model.
      1. Adoration: Praise God for his character and how majestic he is.
      2. Confession: Admit your sins, turn back to God, and state your desire to obey his will.
      3. Thanksgiving: Thank God for his blessings and his work in your life.
      4. Supplication: Present your requests to God.
   B. Bible study: A popular way for reading Scripture daily is the SOAP model.
      1. Scripture: Choose your passage for the day and even read it out loud.
      2. Observation: Consider the main focus of the text, any repeated phrases, who wrote it, and the audience to whom they were writing.
      3. Application: Apply the truths of the passage to your life.
      4. Prayer: Pray through the text and ask the Holy Spirit to reveal the truths about it.
   C. Worship: Worship brings you into the presence of God. Find a style that you connect with the most and use it as a tool for connecting with him.

III. **How do you lead a life that is dedicated to building the kingdom of God?**
   A. Faith: True faith occurs when you act out your trust in God.
      1. You trust in God's sovereignty over your situation.
      2. Faith is found in the confidence you gain when you obey God.
   B. Hope: Hope means placing your confidence in God's character.
      1. You stay focused on Jesus' promise to come back to renew the earth.
      2. You have a perspective of where you are headed in God's story.
   C. Love: You love God with your heart, soul, and mind—and your neighbor.
      1. Loving your neighbor means actually caring for their best interests.
      2. When you love others, you become a reflection of Jesus to them.
      3. God will use you to love the world—and his love will transform the world.

NOTES

"The Bible is a living book that will teach you something new every time you open it."

Discuss [35 MINUTES]

Discuss what you just watched by answering the following questions.

1. It's one thing to *study* the Bible, but it's another thing to actually *apply* its truths to your life. How do you do this? How are you seeking to be a disciple covered in the "dust" of your Rabbi?

2. Ask someone to read aloud Matthew 6:5–13. Prayer is an important holy habit. How does Jesus instruct you to pray? How does this passage encourage you in your current practice of prayer?

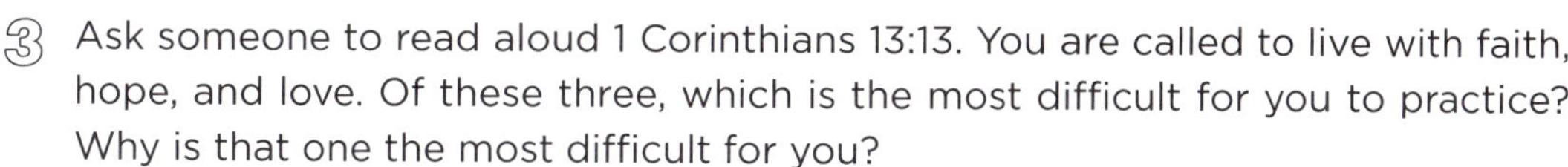

3. Ask someone to read aloud 1 Corinthians 13:13. You are called to live with faith, hope, and love. Of these three, which is the most difficult for you to practice? Why is that one the most difficult for you?

4. Ask someone to read aloud Mark 12:28–34. Why do you think these are the two greatest commands from God? What does it mean to love the Lord your God with all your heart, soul, mind, and strength?

5. Review the list of holy habits. How can you make practicing these habits a priority? Which of these habits do you want to practice more in your life—and why?

Respond [10 MINUTES]

It's easy to talk about faith. It's much harder to practice it. But as you learned in this session, faith is a verb. It is something we *do*, not just something we *have*. And the more we practice faith, the deeper and sturdier our faith will be. Read the passage about faith below and answer the questions that follow.

> [1] Now faith is confidence in what we hope for and assurance about what we do not see. [2] This is what the ancients were commended for. [3] By faith we understand that the universe was formed at God's command, so that what is seen was not made out of what was visible. . . . [6] And without faith it is impossible to please God, because anyone who comes to him must believe that he exists and that he rewards those who earnestly seek him.
>
> **HEBREWS 11:1-3, 6**

How is faith defined in this passage? What do we understand about God by faith?

What two things will you believe about God when you have faith in him?

Pray [10 MINUTES]

When it is time to close this study, take a moment to pray with your group. Thank God for bringing you all together to study his Word. Thank him for the lessons, the questions, and the hard truths. Ask him to continue to grow your faith and your trust in him as you make practicing the holy habits of prayer, Bible study, and worship a priority in your daily life.

SESSION EIGHT

PERSONAL STUDY

You have been on quite a journey in this study. You started back at Creation and explored the covenants that God made with his people. You saw how God called a man named Abraham to be the father of the Jewish race. You witnessed those descendants in captivity in Egypt and watched as God led them into a conquest of the promised land of Canaan. You rode the roller coaster as the Israelites entered a golden age under David and Solomon but ultimately were conquered by foreign powers. You saw how God led a remnant to return to Jerusalem and then brought about the coming of his own Son into the world. You discussed the ministry of Jesus and saw how his death on the cross led to eternal life for everyone who accepts his sacrifice. You watched as the church began to grow and spread. Finally, you took a glimpse at what God has in store for all of his followers during the end times. It's been a dizzying pace! So, in this final personal study, you will slow down a bit to apply all these truths and answer that all-important question, *What does it mean to be a Christian?* As you work through the exercises, continue to write down your responses, reflections, and breakthroughs. If you are reading *The Bible, Simplified* alongside this study, first review chapter 40 in the book.

FINISH THE RACE

STUDY 1 | A Cloud of Witnesses

Hebrews 11 is known as the "Hall of Faith." The author lists many of the heroes of faith—such as Abraham, Sarah, Jacob, Moses, Rahab, Gideon, David, Samuel, and the prophets. He concludes by saying, "Therefore, since we are surrounded by such a great cloud of witnesses, let us throw off everything that hinders and the sin that so easily entangles. And let us run with perseverance the race marked out for us" (12:1).

A "cloud of witnesses" is what keeps our faith going. Think about a race. If you've ever run a marathon, 5K, or other endurance race, you know how you felt in the last half mile. Exhausted. Depleted. Worried you wouldn't finish. In a race, you have people on the sidelines cheering you on—especially at the end. It's amazing what a cheer and shout can do for your energy and stamina. You thought you could not possibly go on, but then you saw a friendly face, and suddenly your feet were moving again.

We need this same encouragement for our faith. Holding on to it isn't easy. Around every corner is a reason to stop believing, to doubt our hope, or to succumb to sin. But when we are surrounded by a loving and encouraging community, we can remain steadfast. We can run that final mile knowing others are either running with us or cheering us on. This is why the author of Hebrews also wrote, "Let us consider how we may spur one another on toward love and good deeds, not giving up meeting together, as some are in the habit of doing, but encouraging one another—and all the more as you see the Day approaching" (10:24–25).

Spur one another on. Don't give up meeting together. Encourage one another. This is how you keep moving ahead in your faith. You surround yourself with a great cloud of witnesses—a community of fellow believers in Christ. You rely on those people to "sharpen" you in your faith, and they rely on you to "sharpen" them (see Proverbs 27:17). You were never meant to live out your faith on your own. You were meant to be part of a collective.

Of course, you aren't called to only hang out with other Christians—quite the opposite! You are called to invite others *into* the faith. But you need other believers to help you stay strong, keep learning, and keep growing. So, if you don't already have this type of community, ask that God would provide you with one. Pray also that he would give you discernment to let those people into your life who will help you increase in faith, hope, and love.

SCRIPTURE: Proverbs 12:15, 26; 13:20; 18:24; 27:6; Ecclesiastes 4:9–10

OBSERVATION

1 Each of these proverbs is known as a "contrastive proverb." They compare the perspective and behavior of a good and wise person with that of wicked and foolish person. In the following table, list the contrasts found in these proverbs as they relate to your friendships.

12:15	The way of fools . . .	but the wise . . .
12:26	The righteous . . .	but the wicked . . .
13:20	Walk with the wise and . . .	for a companion of fools . . .
18:24	One who has unreliable friends . . .	but there is a friend . . .
27:6	Wounds from a friend . . .	but an enemy . . .

2 What does Ecclesiastes 4:9–10 say about the importance of having a good friend?

APPLICATION

3 Who makes up your cloud of witnesses? List three members of your faith community.

PERSON #1	
PERSON #2	
PERSON #3	

4 When has your community helped you strengthen your faith?

5 Is there anything lacking in your faith community? If so, how can you fill this gap?

PRAYER

Lord, thank you for giving me fellow believers to help strengthen my faith. You do not expect me to go this alone. Please give me discernment as I continue to meet with fellow believers. Help me grow closer to those who will lift me up and increase my faith and trust in you. Amen.

WORSHIP • PRAYER • BIBLE STUDY •
Holy Habits

STUDY 2 | The Way to Worship

Worship is one of the essential "holy habits" discussed this week, yet it is frequently misunderstood. When many of us hear the word *worship*, we think about worship services where we sing songs at church. But worship is not confined to music. Worship is a posture of reverence toward God that can be practiced anywhere, any time, and in different ways.

Oswald Chambers, an evangelist and author, defined worship this way:

> Worship is giving God the best that He has given you. Be careful what you do with the best you have. Whenever you get a blessing from God, give it back to Him as a love gift. Take time to meditate before God and offer the blessing back to Him in a deliberate act of worship. If you hoard a thing for yourself, it will turn into spiritual dry rot, as the manna did when it was hoarded. God will never let you hold a spiritual thing for yourself, it has to be given back to Him that He may make it a blessing to others.[22]

Worship is giving God the best that he has given you. Just think about all the things the Lord has given you. He has given you talents, knowledge, wisdom, creativity, resources . . . the list goes on and on. God blesses you every day, but if you choose to hoard those blessings, as Chambers says, those blessings won't be able to bless others. And within you, those blessings will turn into a type of "spiritual dry rot" where they don't even bless you anymore.

When you think about worship in this way, it becomes a daily practice, not just some thing you do in church on Sundays or once in a while at some other type of "worship" event. Maybe God has shown you kindness, so you show kindness to someone else. Maybe God has given you a talent for words, so you write poetry and stories that reflect his goodness. Or maybe God has blessed you with a thriving business, so you donate a portion of your profits to those in your community who need it the most.

Worship is a sharing of blessings. And notice, as Chambers again states, that when you share your blessings, you don't just share a portion of them. No, you share them in full. You give the *best* of your gifts and talents, not holding anything back, because you know the God who gave you those is generous and will give them to you again.

SCRIPTURE: Mark 12:41–44; Luke 21:1–4

OBSERVATION

1. Mark and Luke both relate this story of how Jesus was in the temple in Jerusalem near the end of his ministry watching different people put gifts into the temple treasury. Many of those among the rich threw in large and impressive amounts. What did the poor widow give in this story?

2. In Mark's account, Jesus called his disciples over to him to teach them an important lesson about giving to God. What did Jesus say was significant about the poor widow's gift?

3. How does this story reflect the way that we should worship God?

APPLICATION

4 Oswald Chambers wrote, "Be careful what you do with the best you have. . . . If you hoard a thing for yourself, it will turn into spiritual dry rot." Have you witnessed this in your life? If so, explain what happened as a result.

5 Think about three blessings God has recently given you and write them in the chart below. Then brainstorm how you could share those blessings with others.

BLESSING	How I can share this blessing with others
1.	
2.	
3.	

PRAYER

Father of all blessings, thank you for the gifts you have given me. Please show me how I can bless others in the way that you have blessed me. Give me a heart for worship every day. May I live each day worshiping you. Amen.

HOPEFULNESS

STUDY 3 | Confident Hope

For a story to make the news, it must be considered "newsworthy." Journalists abide by eight tenets to make a story newsworthy: (1) timeliness, (2) proximity, (3) importance, (4) interest, (5) conflict, (6) sensationalism, (7) prominence, and (8) novelty.[23] What word doesn't make the list? *Hopefulness.*

Hopeful stories are typically not considered newsworthy. In fact, "generally speaking, editors deem bad news more newsworthy than good news."[24] No wonder it's so difficult to hope in this day and age. Not much hope is being spread.

This is why it's important to read the Bible. While God's Word provides benefits like knowledge, wisdom, and understanding, it also provides a daily dose of *hope*. And this hope is not fleeting or naïve. It is a secure hope that leads to deeper faith. As you read during the group time this week in Hebrews 11:1, "Faith is confidence in what we hope for and assurance about what we do not see." While the hope you place in the things of this world will often let you down, your hope in God never will.

You know what it's like to get your hopes up only to find those hopes dashed. It makes you cautious about hoping for anything again in the future. But as a child of God, you don't have to guard your heart in this way. You are free to hope because the message of the Bible is clear:

> God's kingdom is coming.
> You are saved through Jesus.
> You will spend eternity with Christ and your heavenly Father.

Near the end of Paul's letter to the church in Rome, he wrote, "May the God of hope fill you with all joy and peace as you trust in him, so that you may overflow with hope by the power of the Holy Spirit" (Romans 15:13). This was more than just a closing platitude. Paul understood the world often seems bleak. This is why we need the God of hope to fill us with his joy and peace—so we literally overflow with hope.

We find this hope in the Bible. So, the next time it seems as if there is no light at the end of the tunnel, pull out this great work of literature and open its pages. And keep turning to it again and again so that God can keep filling you with hope. For he will never disappoint you or let you down.

SCRIPTURE: Romans 15:1–13

APPLICATION

1. Paul urges his readers to bear with one another (see verses 1–2). He then draws on the example of Christ, who "did not please himself," and quotes from Psalm 69:9: "The insults of those who insult you have fallen on me" (verse 3).

   What does Paul say is the purpose of verses like these "written in the past" (verse 4)?

   What was Paul's prayer for the believers in Rome (see verses 5–6)?

   What were the believers to remember when it came to accepting others (see verse 7)?

2. How does Paul use Scripture in verses 9–12 to guide the Roman believers? How do you think this would have encouraged them to accept one another?

APPLICATION

3 On a scale of 1 to 10, how hopeful do you feel today?

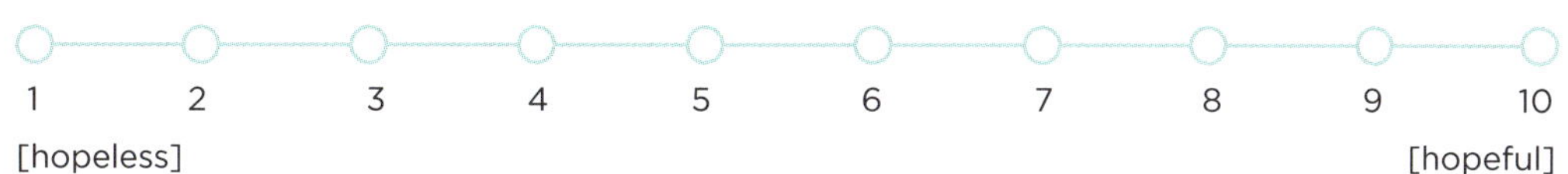

4 How have you experienced hope in this study as you have gone through the Bible?

5 Where do you need more hope in your life right now? How would you like God to fill you with his joy and peace so that you are overflowing with hope?

PRAYER

God of hope, fill me with joy and peace as I learn to trust in you. Fill me with hope by the power of your Spirit. As I continue to study your Word and apply it to my life, may I overflow with godly hope so that I can share that hope with others. In Jesus' name, I pray. Amen.

WRAP IT UP

Connect with a fellow group member one last time to discuss some of the insights from this session. Use any of the following prompts to help guide your discussion.

1. Who is someone in your life who models faith, hope, and love? What impact has this person had on you?

2. Of the holy habits discussed in this session—prayer, study, and worship—which is hardest for you to practice? Which one is easiest? Why?

3. How do you plan to make studying the Bible a daily priority after this study has concluded? What are some practical and sustainable habits you could start putting into place today?

4. What are some of the biggest lessons that you will take away from this study about the Bible, God, and yourself?

Don't let the fact this is the end of *this* study on the Bible signal the end of *your* study of the Bible. Discuss with your group what studies you might want to go through next and when you plan on meeting together again to study God's Word.

Leader's Guide

Thank you for your willingness to lead your group through this study! What you've chosen to do is valuable and will make a difference in the lives of others. *The Bible, Simplified* is an eight-session Bible study built around video content and small-group interaction. As the group leader, imagine yourself as the host of a party. Your job is to take care of your guests by managing the details so that when your guests arrive, they can focus on one another and on the interaction around the topic for that session.

Your role as the group leader is not to answer all the questions or reteach the content—the video, book, and study guide will do most of that work. Your job is to guide the experience and cultivate your small group into a connected and engaged community. This will make it a place for members to process, question, and reflect—not necessarily to receive more instruction. There are several elements in this leader's guide that will help you as you structure your study and reflection time, so be sure to follow along and take advantage of each one.

Before You Begin

Before your first meeting, make sure the group members have a copy of this study guide. You can also hand out the study guides at your first meeting and give the members some time to look over the material and ask any preliminary questions. Also, make sure the group members are aware they have access to the streaming videos at any time by following the instructions provided with this guide. During your first meeting, ask the members to provide their names, phone numbers, and email addresses so that you can keep in touch with them.

Generally, the ideal size for a group is eight to ten people, which will ensure everyone has enough time to participate in discussions. If you have more people, you might want to break up the main group into smaller subgroups. Encourage those who show up at the first meeting to commit to attending the duration of the study, as this will help the group members get to know one another, create stability for the group, and help you know how best to prepare to lead the participants through the material.

Each session begins with an opening reflection in the Welcome section. The questions that follow in the Connect section serve as icebreakers to get the group members thinking about the session topic. In the rest of the study, it's generally not a good idea to have everyone answer every question—a free-flowing discussion is more desirable. But with the icebreaker question, you can go around the circle and ask each person to respond. Encourage shy people to share, but don't force them.

At your first meeting, let the group members know that each session also contains a personal study section they can use to continue to engage with the content until the next meeting. While doing this section is optional, it will help the participants cement the concepts presented during the group study time and help them work their way through the Bible.

Let them know that if they choose to do so, they can watch the video for the next session by accessing the streaming code provided with this study guide. Invite them to bring any questions and insights to your next meeting, especially if they had a breakthrough moment or didn't understand something.

Preparation for Each Session

As the leader, there are a few things that you should do to best prepare for each group meeting:

- **Read through the session.** This will help you become more familiar with the content and know how to structure the discussion times.
- **Decide how the videos will be used.** Determine whether you want the members to watch the videos ahead of time or together as a group.
- **Decide which questions you want to discuss.** You may not be able to get through all the questions, so look over the discussion questions provided in each session and mark which ones you definitely want to cover.
- **Be familiar with the questions that you want to discuss.** When the group meets, you'll be watching the clock, so be familiar with the questions that you selected.
- **Pray for your group.** Pray for your group members and ask God to lead them as they study his Word and listen to his Spirit.

Keep in mind as you lead the discussion time that in many cases there will be no one "right" answer to the questions. Answers will vary, especially when the group members are being asked to share their personal experiences.

Structuring the Discussion Time

You will need to determine how long you want your meetings to last so that you can plan your time accordingly. Suggested times for each section have been provided in this guide, and if you adhere to these times, your group will meet for ninety minutes. However, many groups like to meet for two hours. If this describes your particular group, follow the times listed in the right-hand column of the chart given below.

SECTION	90 Minutes	120 Minutes
CONNECT (discuss one or more of the opening questions for the session)	15 minutes	20 minutes
WATCH (watch the teaching material together and take notes)	20 minutes	20 minutes
DISCUSS (discuss the study questions you selected ahead of time)	35 minutes	50 minutes
RESPOND (write down key takeaways)	10 minutes	15 minutes
PRAY (pray together and dismiss)	10 minutes	15 minutes

As the group leader, it is up to you to keep track of the time and keep things on schedule. You might want to set a timer for each segment so both you and the group members know when the time is up. (There are some good phone apps for timers that play a gentle chime or other pleasant sound instead of a disruptive noise.)

Don't be concerned if group members are quiet or slow to share. People are often quiet when they are pulling together their ideas, and this might be a new experience for some of them. Ask a question and let it hang in the air until someone shares. You can then say, "Thank you. What about others?"

Group Dynamics

Leading a group through *The Bible, Simplified* will prove to be highly rewarding to you and your group members. But you still may encounter challenges along the way! Discussions can get off track. Members may not be sensitive to the needs and ideas of others. Some might worry they will be expected to talk about matters that make them feel awkward. Others may express comments that result in disagreements. To help ease this strain on you and the group, consider the following ground rules:

- When someone raises a question or comment off the main topic, suggest you deal with it another time, or, if you feel led to go in that direction, let the group know you will be spending some time discussing it.

- If someone asks a question that you don't know how to answer, admit it and move on. At your discretion, feel free to invite group members to comment on questions that call for personal experience.

- If you find that one or two people are dominating the discussion time, direct a few questions to others. Outside the main group time, ask the more dominating members to help you draw out the quieter ones. Work to make them part of the solution instead of part of the problem.

- When a disagreement occurs, encourage the group members to process the matter in love. Encourage those on opposite sides to restate what they heard the other side say about the matter, and then invite each side to evaluate if that perception is accurate. Lead the group in examining other Scriptures related to the topic and look for common ground.

When any of these issues arise, encourage your group members to follow these words from Scripture: "Love one another" (John 13:34); "If it is possible, as far as it depends on you, live at peace with everyone" (Romans 12:18); and, "Everyone should be quick to listen, slow to speak and slow to become angry" (James 1:19). This will make your group time more rewarding and beneficial for everyone who attends.

Thank you for taking the time to lead your group through *The Bible, Simplified*. You are making a difference in your group members' lives and having an impact on their journey toward gaining a better understanding of God's Word and learning what it means to live as a Christian.

Notes

1. A. W. Tozer, cited in *The Quotable Tozer*, edited by James L. Snyder (Minneapolis, MN: Bethany House, 2018), 36.
2. Billy Graham, cited in *Decision Magazine*, July/August 2006, https://www.billygraham.ca/100-quotes-from-billy-graham/.
3. F. F. Bruce, et al, *The Origin of the Bible* (Carol Stream, IL: Tyndale House Publishers, 2020).
4. Bodie Hodge and Dr. Terry Mortenson, "Did Moses Write Genesis?" Answers in Genesis, June 28, 2011, https://answersingenesis.org/bible-characters/moses/did-moses-write-genesis/.
5. Craig S. Keener, editor, *The IVP Bible Background Commentary: New Testament* (Lisle, IL: Inter-Varsity Press, 1993), 290.
6. See "Recommended Resources for Further Study" in *The Bible, Simplified* for additional options.
7. Paul J. Zak, "Why Your Brain Loves Good Storytelling," Harvard Business Review, October 28, 2014, https://hbr.org/2014/10/why-your-brain-loves-good-storytelling.
8. Zach Windahl, *The Bible, Simplified* (Nashville, TN: Nelson Books, 2025), 30.
9. Windahl, *The Bible, Simplified*, 36.
10. John H. Walton, Victor H. Matthews, and Mark W. Chavalas, *The IVP Bible Background Commentary: Old Testament* (Downers Grove, IL: InterVarsity Press, 2000), 53.
11. The Bible Project, "Holiness," accessed January 16, 2025, https://bibleproject.com/explore/video/holiness/.
12. "Wisdom," *King James Bible Dictionary*, accessed January 20, 2025, https://kingjamesbibledictionary.com/Dictionary/wisdom.
13. N. T. Wright, "Why Don't the Gospels Match?" N. T. Wright Online, https://www.ntwrightonline.org/why-dont-the-gospels-match/.
14. Lee Strobel, *The Case for Christ: A Journalist's Personal Investigation of the Evidence for Jesus* (Grand Rapids, MI: Zondervan, 2016).
15. Craig S. Keener, editor, *The IVP Bible Background Commentary: New Testament* (Downers Grove, IL: InterVarsity Press, 1993), 55.
16. Keener, *The IVP Bible Background Commentary: New Testament*, 55.
17. The Bible Project, "Gospel and Acts 3," https://bibleproject.com/explore/video/gospel-acts-3/.
18. Thomas R. Hatina, "Rome and Its Provinces," in *The World of the New Testament*, edited by Joel B. Green and Lee Martin McDonald (Grand Rapids, MI: Baker Academic, 2013), 567.
19. Hatina, in *The World of the New Testament*, 567.
20. Zach Windahl, *The Bible, Simplified* (Nashville, TN: Nelson Books, 2025), 264.
21. Alan F. Johnson, *The Expositor's Bible Commentary: Revelation* (Grand Rapids, MI: Zondervan Academic, 2006). 619.
22. Oswald Chambers, "Worship," *My Utmost for His Highest*, December 15, 2024, https://utmost.org/classic/worship-classic/.
23. Purdue Online Writing Lab, "Components of Newsworthiness," Purdue University, https://owl.purdue.edu/owl/subject_specific_writing/journalism_and_journalistic_writing/components_of_newsworthiness.html.
24. Purdue Online Writing Lab, "Components of Newsworthiness."

Also Available from

Zach Windahl

Available wherever books are sold.

About Zach Windahl

Zach Windahl is an author and content creator focused on helping people grow in their faith. He is the author of several books, including *The Bible Study: A One-Year Study of the Bible and How It Relates to You*. He lives in Orlando, Florida, with his wife, Gisela. You can connect with Zach on social media at @ZachWindahl or at www.ZachWindahl.com.

From the Publisher

GREAT STUDIES

ARE EVEN BETTER WHEN THEY'RE SHARED!

Help others find this study:

- Post a review at your favorite online bookseller.
- Post a picture on a social media account and share why you enjoyed it.
- Send a note to a friend who would also love it—or, better yet, go through it with them!

Thanks for helping others grow their faith!